COME UP HERE!

COME UP HERE!
A Journey into God's Glory

CONNIE HUNTER-URBAN
Foreword by Cheryel Tarter

RESOURCE *Publications* · Eugene, Oregon

COME UP HERE!
A Journey into God's Glory

Copyright © 2025 Connie Hunter-Urban. All rights reserved. Except for brief quotations in critical publications or reviews, no part of this book may be reproduced in any manner without prior written permission from the publisher. Write: Permissions, Wipf and Stock Publishers, 199 W. 8th Ave., Suite 3, Eugene, OR 97401.

Resource Publications
An Imprint of Wipf and Stock Publishers
199 W. 8th Ave., Suite 3
Eugene, OR 97401

www.wipfandstock.com

PAPERBACK ISBN: 979-8-3852-4088-3
HARDCOVER ISBN: 979-8-3852-4089-0
EBOOK ISBN: 979-8-3852-4090-6

02/14/25

John said, "After these things I looked, and behold, a door standing open in heaven. And the first voice which I heard was like a trumpet speaking with me, saying, 'Come up here, and I will show you things which must take place after this'" (Rev. 4:1). Most Christians are content to live at "see" level where they only dwell in what they can see around them. The Lord has so much more. As we travel through our Christian journey, we must always be going higher in Him toward the realm of the glory.

Contents

Foreword by Cheryel Tarter	ix
Acknowledgments	xi
Introduction	xiii

PART ONE | MY CALL

CHAPTER ONE: Call to *Higher*	3
CHAPTER TWO: Higher	7

PART TWO | EZEKIEL'S JOURNEY

CHAPTER THREE: Ezekiel, the Glory	17
CHAPTER FOUR: Angels	26
CHAPTER FIVE: Ezekiel, the Call and Preparation	35
CHAPTER SIX: Worship	40
CHAPTER SEVEN: Ezekiel, the Commission	51
CHAPTER EIGHT: Count the Cost	66

PART THREE | GLORY PURPOSES

CHAPTER NINE: Reasons for the Glory: Redemptive Names	75
CHAPTER TEN: Prophetic Actions	86
CHAPTER ELEVEN: Reasons for the Glory: Other Purposes	92

Contents

PART FOUR | FROM GLORY TO GLORY

CHAPTER TWELVE: The Story Is Unfolding 107
Epilogue 139
Endnotes 141
Appendix #1 145
Appendix #2 146
Appendix #3 147
Appendix #4 148
Appendix #5 149
Appendix #6 150
Appendix #7 151
Appendix #8 152
Appendix #9 153
Appendix #10 154
Appendix #11 155
Appendix #12 156
Bibliography 157

Foreword

Psalm 42:7 declares: "Deep calls unto deep!" Deep things of God call unto the deep places in our spirit man. Who will answer this call? The depth of the riches of God's mysteries, and unfolding revelations of His Glory flow ONLY to a deep, unfettered place of surrendered intimacy in Christ.

Read these pages from Connie Hunter-Urban's heart, as she reveals encounters from the Glory Realm. Allow yourself to hear God's personal call to the fathomless billows of God's Spirit. Go where you've never been in Him before. Open your heart to leave the familiar and go into the unknown, for by faith Christ will usher you into the deep places of God. You will never be the same.

    Apostle Cheryel Tarter, Revivalist
    PhD Theology
    Covenant Bible College
    Hamilton, OH

Acknowledgments

I would like to thank the following people for their support:

The Lord, who sent me on this higher journey and led me step-by-step.

My husband Wade, who always encourages me to do whatever Holy Spirit leads me to do.

My friend, Margie, who stepped up without hesitation to edit my wordiness.

My Zoom morning worship group, who have been faithful to hear tremendous revelations from Holy Spirit.

My friend Curtis who passed away during the writing of this book. He was truly a friend and brother, who, in his own way, showed that he was proud of each book I wrote. I miss you, Bro!

Introduction

For the entire planet, events of 2020 were horrific. Though Covid wreaked havoc, this type of worldwide crisis wasn't new. History has been fraught with carnage associated with epidemics and pandemics. In Rome in AD 250–271, 5,000 per day died in the Plague of Cyprian. The Black Death in 1346–1353 is estimated to have killed more than half of Europe's citizens.[1] From H1N1 to polio to AIDS and others, all affected many, and one result transpired—the world changed. The same was true of Covid. As 2020 proceeded with modifications in lives and the Christian world, attendance dropped in churches. However though quarantines affected turnouts at churches, many changed the disaster into a blessing. They found alternate ways to work for and serve the Kingdom while reaching people around the world.

With stay-at-home orders in place, my husband Wade and I persisted with ministry by other methods. At the first of the year, we'd begun our Discipleship Class. After we could no longer meet together, we had teachings and multiple prayer times, using Zoom and Facebook Live in lieu of in-person gatherings. In the summer, one of my nieces suffered multiple seizures each day, so we needed to pray in one accord as a family. My sisters and I initiated a Sunday afternoon Zoom prayer meeting so geographical distance between us wasn't an issue. The number of her seizures went down drastically after the first prayer session, and many prayers for her and other family members' situations were answered.

The Lord is continuing to resolve other needs we've addressed as we still intercede—for healings, renewals, deliverances, miracles. We've perceived angelic presences during these meetings. Once, I even felt an angel take my wrist and put it on the monitor as a point of contact for whom we were interceding. I love when Joseph told his brothers that what they had

---

1. Jarus, "Worst Epidemics," livescience.com.

Introduction

meant for bad, God used for good (see Gen. 45:5–7). Covid and quarantines were from the pit of hell. God utilized them to show us new tools with which we could work for the Kingdom.

In December, the church we attend called for a one-week fast to seek God's direction for the following year. I'd also felt led to pursue ministry focus for 2021. Because of this, my husband and I adopted a regimen of less television, intentional fasting, increased Bible reading with prayer as my morning's first fruits, and regular worship at home. We set aside time to pray together in one accord to find the Lord's will for us. Almost immediately, He responded. As we dedicated more quality time to Him, He showed us one thing He wanted us to do: "Get back to basics."

That word applied to more than one aspect of our ministry. The year before, we taught Discipleship Class twice from my book, *God's Plan for Our Success, Nehemiah's Way.* Those teachings instructed the newly saved or those wanting to understand what to expect as their journeys progressed toward destiny. Classes had gone well, but I knew Holy Spirit was leading us to approach the beginning-of-the-year Discipleship Class differently. Wade and I agreed that in the first session, we should teach about Holy Spirit's gifts. That was part of returning to our ministry basics. We would use our co-authored book, *Your Holy Spirit Arsenal,* as the text. We knew the Lord had spoken, but we weren't sure how to proceed to revisit our roots. He soon revealed direction concerning another ministry aspect.

Twenty-five years earlier, He'd led us to teach others about Holy Spirit's operation. We'd done that while evangelizing, pastoring, and hosting a Bible study in our home. Those meetings had evolved into our Times of Refreshing services, which were to be an outlet for people to learn to use their gifts. After those gatherings had grown, we'd left our house for a bigger venue. Over time, though, location wasn't the only aspect that had changed. At first, we'd taught about the gifts, and Holy Spirit had accomplished great demonstrations of power—intense travail, amazing miracles, prolific revelations. Now, those meetings had become less about Holy Spirit taking over but more like a regular service—worship, preaching, ministry. Revelations and operating in Holy Spirit's gifts still occurred; but usually Wade, a few others, and I shared those. The Lord wanted us to return to teaching and letting other people hone their gifts, too.

Instructing those who were unfamiliar in Holy Spirit's baptism was crucial because their gifts' operation was new territory for many. We wanted to provide a safe place to grow and make mistakes that accompany

Introduction

learning. With these revelations, I thought Holy Spirit had shown us our complete direction for the year, but His will continued to become clearer as we progressed. Instead of a once-a-month service, He led us to use the first part of our weekly classes to teach about one of the gifts and the second half to allow those attending to operate in the gift we'd taught. As a result, we saw much excitement and growth. These revelations and results made me feel I was walking extremely close to God, growing deeper myself each day. I was wrong.

We needed to take others not only deeper, but higher. A difference exists between those concepts. Both indicate growth, but deeper is learning more about God's precepts and discovering foundational truths. Without firm groundwork, a person can't go higher. Higher is experiencing new occurrences, often the supernatural. In this book, when I use the word "higher" as a description of where I wanted to go, I don't italicize. When I use it to designate the concept of climbing to another spiritual plane, I italicize *higher*.

No matter where we are in our growth in the Lord, we can all go higher. I wrote this book to share my own path to *higher*. A large number of scriptures refers to Ezekiel's first three chapters, where his visions parallel my own *higher* journey. I also mention John often because his "Revelation" book corresponds closely to Ezekiel's. I've learned and experienced much through their words and my own *higher* journey. Join me as I share my higher growth expedition accomplished through the Bible, Holy Spirit, supernatural experiences, and abundant revelations. I know that if you also want to climb higher in the Lord, you can, too.

PART ONE

MY CALL

CHAPTER ONE
Call to *Higher*

My parents' relationship with the Lord was on a higher plane than most. Because of our experiences, we knew before my childhood that profound occurrences in the glory realm are real and amazing. When I was in elementary school, classes had been canceled because an ice storm blanketed the already-snowy ground. Excited to have a day off, my siblings and I enjoyed the wondrous beauty of ice-covered trees, bushes, gutters, and everything else, even electric lines. With all of us at home, Mom was likely ready for a break when we asked to sled on the hill and frozen creek by our house. We bundled carefully, trudged gingerly across the yard, and arrived expectantly at the slope.

On the hill, the thick, frozen covering created a slick and exciting lane. This entertained us for quite a while. We were slipping, sliding, and sledding with the pent-up energy of healthy children when Mom shouted from the kitchen door, "You guys come home!"

We were far enough away that we could've claimed we didn't hear, stayed a while longer, and raced a few more times down the glassy hillside. However her no-nonsense tone told us to come at once. We later discovered that while she'd been doing devotions, Holy Spirit put a word inside her: "Bring the kids into the house. NOW!"

Mom always said that when revelations come, you "know in your knower" they're real and important. This time, her knower said, "NOW!"

Grumbling, we'd trudged home as fast as the slick-coated grass and our hand-me-down boots would allow. As she swung open the kitchen door, we huddled in a mass, awaiting our turn to file inside. Before we could all go in, though, we heard a sound like a harsh, bass drum. We spun around and witnessed an appalling sight. Near the hill's crest, where we'd been sledding, ice-coated electric lines had fallen into our racing lanes. Prolonged, intense burning created a dip in the hill where fiery current etched a reminder of its power and danger. For all the years we lived there, that depression in the ground said more. For each subsequent sledding session, the groove reminded us God would go before us and save our families. Many examples in our lives demonstrate Father's care for His kids, whether the need is simple or dire.

THE FLOOD

The confidence I learned in childhood assured me that God had more power and wonder than most people realize. That knowledge would be part of my higher journey, and it started with a dream. Wade and I had maneuvered through pared-down holiday celebrations. Covid had lingered and hit many homes, including ours. We looked forward to a new year when we could catapult into the new/old direction God was impressing upon us. As we prepared for Holy Spirit class, the Lord had other plans for this new direction. In January, I had this dream:

> *We were at our home, but the house was sometimes ours in Indiana and sometimes my childhood Ohio home. Outside, a deluge of rain pelted the house. For some reason, we lived in the Indiana basement. My daughter Jill was about three years old, and her bed was located in that sub-ground level. Suddenly water gushed in from the bottom of the walls, the level rising fast and ferociously. We needed to get to a higher place quickly, so I grabbed Jill and carried her upstairs. Wade followed as we climbed. The scene changed to the Ohio living room. I didn't see much furniture, but I noticed a piano. I knew we'd be safe, but the basement would need to be fixed later.*

I gleaned several messages from the dream. Regardless of how high we've operated in gifts of the Spirit, we've been living in a lower level in Him. We're going to be forced higher. Water represents Holy Spirit, so He'll be the Tool to compel us upward. We needed to rise to the next level and protect our child, which was our ministry. The Lord had said what He would reveal several other times. Carrying our ministry higher would be my responsibility, and worship (the piano) would be a major part.

The day after the dream, someone texted and said Holy Spirit had been telling her that He's sending a spiritual tsunami. That's the flood in my dream! Several years ago, Holy Spirit had spoken into my spirit: "A gentle ebbing." At that time, amazing signs and wonders had occurred and were still happening; but God was saying that compared to what the future would bring, this was a gentle ebbing. I believe that's even truer now. We'd been satisfied with where we were in the Lord when much more is available. The gentle ebbing hasn't propelled us significantly higher, so we should prepare for the Holy Spirit tsunami that's coming.

A few days after this revelation, the Lord reinforced His message. During worship, I saw a vision with the same *higher* message:

> *I stood in front of a platform like a concert riser. A few others milled around, but I don't know if they were angels or people. I was at the bottom of the steps; Jesus was at the top. He smiled and extended His hands in front of His body, welcoming me higher. His eyes were saying, "Connie, come up here where I am!" His loving gaze amazed me, as His hands reached tenderly toward me.*

My dream's message was now repeated in a vision. I needed to seek then step into *higher*.

A WAYS TO GO

My dream and vision spoke unmistakably: I should be more elevated in Him. Though the Lord wanted me to come to where He was, this vision was saying I hadn't yet arrived on the first step. I didn't know where to start. When I dream of the Ohio house, it represents either my foundations in the Lord (i.e., Holy Spirit) or Wade's and my pastoring season. By the next year, it could have also meant an actual house in Ohio when we moved about a half mile from my childhood home. In many of my dreams, a child symbolizes ministries. Jill represented a specific ministry, and her age in the dream meant something, too. Three years before, our co-authored book, *Your Holy Spirit Arsenal,* had been re-released by Destiny Image. I needed to rely on Holy Spirit's work in our ministry as we prepared for teaching and my quest to *higher*.

I always knew that Holy Spirit would take us higher, but the Lord's message to me that I wasn't yet to the first floor or first step humbled me. My dream and multiple visions then and later said, "Go higher!" Our parents had exposed us to Holy Spirit's gifts at home, in church, or at Faith Healers' services where we witnessed numerous, amazing miracles. I've operated in the gifts since before I was a teenager. I've sat in His presence often and have seen astounding signs, wonders, and revelations. Because of my background, I thought I was deeper in the Spirit than most. However, God was saying I haven't yet scratched the surface. I had to get more deliberate about *higher*. Though my background had made me who I was now, I couldn't dwell on what had happened in the past or stay in my house of complacency. I should push ahead to reach my destiny, my calling from God. I desperately desired to travel upward to a new *higher* level of experience.

CHAPTER TWO

Higher

WHAT *HIGHER* LOOKS LIKE

In our worship and prayer times, Wade and I linger, soak in His presence, and then share what Holy Spirit has spoken to us. One night, I commented, "The Lord wants to take us higher, but what does *higher* look like?" We admitted we didn't know. The following night, His powerful presence erupted. It was the *Shekinah* glory, a "visible manifestation of God on earth, whose presence is portrayed through a natural occurrence."[1] The Hebrew word *Shekinah* means "dwelling" or "one who dwells."[2] We're created as a "habitation of God through the Spirit" (Eph. 2:22). He dwells in and with us.

Though not actually found biblically, the word *Shekinah* was first used by Jewish rabbis during the period between Old and New Testaments. It's derived from a Hebrew word, *shākan*, which means "to reside or permanently stay."[3] The Lord doesn't want occasional visits with us. He wants to stay permanently and constantly! Moses experienced God's presence on Mount Sinai (see Exod. 19:20). It also appeared in a pillar of cloud by day and fire by night (see Exod. 13:21–22). *Shekinah* is the flame indicating His presence.[4]

The night after I voiced that question about *higher*, Wade and I soaked in His presence, and several examples of *higher* came. Someone or something touched the fourth toe on my right foot while I sat at the piano. I wasn't sure what that particular toe represented; but as I later read "Ezekiel," the number four had much significance. The Bible alludes to toes' importance. Aaron consecrated himself and his sons by putting ram's blood on their clothing and parts of their body, including the right ear, thumb of the right hand, and big toe of the right foot (see Exod. 29:19–21). Those locations signify that they'd hear only God's Word, perform priests' duties in a right manner, and walk in righteousness.[5]

That night, after I moved onto the couch, I couldn't lift my hands, arms, or legs, just my tingling fingers. As I basked in that intense presence, I asked Wade to sit beside me on the couch so I could lay my fingers on him and me. When I could raise my arms, I touched my forehead and discovered thick oil which I also rubbed on our heads. We prayed together, not knowing why God had brought that sign and wonder. During the night, I was awakened when Wade cried out. In the morning, he told me a pop had gone off in his head. In our *higher* moment with tingling fingers and oil-laden foreheads, the Lord had spared my husband from injury or death.

Wade recognized that sensation because the same thing had occurred a few years earlier. As we hosted a Holy Spirit conference, several people felt led to pray for him. My sister had dreamed he had a stroke. Others shared revelations about the enemy's planned attacks against him. We all knew that God reveals danger in advance so we can pray for victory, not fear what's coming. At the conference's end, we created a prayer tunnel. As people inched through that line, many needs were met by Holy Spirit's power. When Wade went through the lines as the last person, a substantial anointing had pervaded the building. The following night, he'd experienced the first pop in his head. All those years before, he'd suffered a mini stroke which left lingering symptoms. The enemy had planned a catastrophe then and now, but it didn't happen. This time, not only did the stroke not succeed, but Wade had no residual symptoms. That's *higher*.

PRAYER CLOTHS

We rejoiced because God had gone before us both times. Several days later, Holy Spirit would lead me to use another powerful tool which brought an answer—prayer cloths. When Paul ministered, God did many miracles through his hands. Because he couldn't lay those powerful tools on everyone, others took handkerchiefs and aprons that had touched his body and gave them to those who were suffering. People were healed and delivered through that simple point of contact (see Acts 19:11–12). Today, those cloths made from garments are still a valuable tool as God uses them to bring answers to people as we anoint and pray over the cloths. Miracles have occurred after a prayer cloth was pinned to a pillow or clothing or carried in a wallet.

A few days after I'd anointed Wade's head, we were again sitting in His presence after worship. I felt abundant oil return to my forehead, and I realized its purpose. A few days earlier, I'd been led by the Spirit to anoint prayer cloths to give to ladies with conception problems. I'd smeared oil on those cloths and prayed over them myself and then with Wade, but I didn't feel I was supposed to send them yet. I laid them on a cookie sheet and set them by the piano to become saturated with the glory that entered during worship. That night, I understood the last step for those cloths. Though I'd anointed them with bottled oil, I added that thick heavenly oil from my forehead. I also wiped tears onto each small square as our glory time led into travail.

I sent the cloths to ladies on our prayer list, along with a note explaining the process the Lord had led me through. One of them, a pastor's wife, had been desperate for a child after a miscarriage. Because I barely knew her, I wasn't sure if she believed in prayer cloths, so I hesitated. However, I obeyed Holy Spirit and messaged to see if she wanted one. She immediately responded and gave me her address. I didn't see or hear about her for a while. Near the end of the year, she posted Facebook pictures of her new son. When I checked the date I'd contacted her, I rejoiced. Her beautiful, perfect, baby was born ten months after I sent the prayer cloth! That's *higher*.

MORE GLORY HAPPENINGS

The next Sunday, I shared the *higher* experiences with my sisters on Zoom prayer time. When I'd first shared my *higher* dream with them, they were touched by the Lord's communication about going higher in Him. All of them had said they wanted that *higher* walk, especially Anita, my youngest sister. Since the beginning of these meetings more than six months earlier, her hunger for God had been renewed. Though she'd always been a Christian, her fervor had waned. The day we'd committed to *higher*, she cried. I saw that from her often during subsequent meetings.

In mid-March, she texted a video then called. She explained, "My security alarm went off the other night when I'd just gotten into bed. I looked at the foyer video, and this is what I saw. Watch at the left side from the start and see what you think."

I hit the play button, and I observed a remarkable sight. An angelic orb began at the left side of the picture and traveled across the screen. That orb was not only obvious to Anita and me, but it had enough substance to set off her alarm. God has "raised us up together, and made us sit together in the heavenly places in Christ Jesus" (Eph. 2:6). To get higher into those heavenly places, we must be raised higher, and Anita was being taken higher in His glory. That wasn't the last time orbs were recorded on her security camera.

ORBS

Orbs weren't a new concept for us. When we were first in ministry, as Wade preached, I'd see lights move slowly through the congregation and stop over someone. As we ministered to that person, Holy Spirit showed Himself mighty each time. Those lights were probably orbs I saw with my human eye. At that point, we hadn't heard the term "orb." Years later, as we taught about glory manifestations, people were curious about them. Some had read that teens have parties to chase them. By the way, those aren't heavenly but demonic, and I wasn't surprised they were around. Whatever the Lord gives, the enemy counterfeits. Angelic orbs, however, are astounding. When they show up, angels are present for a purpose.

Though controversy exists about what those circles of light are, I'm convinced they truly are angels, usually unseen by the human eye (see Appendix #1). Orbs have always been there, but the invention of digital cameras revealed them. More than twenty years ago, we'd seen these in pictures for the first time. Now, we witness them often. In reality, "we do not look at the things which are seen, but at the things which are not seen. For the things which are seen are temporary, but the things which are not seen are eternal" (2 Cor. 4:18). These phenomena we usually don't see with our natural eyes are more real and lasting than what we perceive in this earthly realm. Though the natural eye doesn't see them often, angels are real, plentiful, and eternal.

MORE *HIGHER*

The night after Anita sent her first orb video, we settled in to worship. I'd brought my phone and placed it on the coffee table to record. Sometimes when I worship, the Lord gives me new songs I want to remember. This time, I again forgot to turn it on. After I'd finished what I'd planned to sing, I thought about the phone and started a video. I continued worshiping, this time with simple words of adoration—"I love You . . . I need You . . . You're so very worthy . . . ." With those declarations to our Father, Wade and I could feel His profuse presence permeate the room even greater than usual, due to the prolonged gate of worship we sat in.

After soaking a while in His presence, I snapped pictures around the room. In those photos, beams of light filled with faces stretched from floor to ceiling around the piano. In one live shot, an intense flash of light appeared in the frame (see Appendix #2–#3). As we watched the video, we saw other amazing occurrences. During some parts of worship, darkened areas above my head turned lighter. At times, sparks of light streaked past my face or above my head. When I enlarged those pictures, they were small orbs, and some had faces. We were amazed, but that wasn't the last of those occurrences. On multiple occasions during worship before our streaming program, pictures were filled with abundant orbs and beams.

The night after I saw those faces, I slept little, not understanding the implications of what I'd seen. I woke up early Sunday. Wade and I weren't going to church that day because we were picking up our daughter and granddaughter from the airport. As I did devotions, I texted Anita and said I needed to tell her what had happened the night before. When she responded, I called and told her what transpired the previous night. I texted my pictures, and we looked through them together, talked about them, and zoomed in on the many faces. She texted a video of her own of something that was happening right then at her Arizona house.

"Do you see glitter in front of my TV?" I had told her about gold dust falling often with the glory. It was usually small and fine, so tiny that when it first appeared, we had to be shown what it looked like as it covered our hands or other places on our bodies and clothes. Her video wasn't that. Large, multi-colored glitter flakes floated lazily toward the floor (see Appendix #4). The sight astonished us. Anita and I were in awe of how God was taking us higher. Holy Spirit spoke to Anita to worship Him immediately because we were in His presence. Wonder lingered with us, but that wasn't the last time *God's* presence invaded *our* presence.

PART ONE | MY CALL

THE CONTRADICTION

When we make gains in our journey, often the opposite of our goal happens. My daughter and granddaughter came to visit. Because they were here, we didn't worship regularly. At one of the many activities we planned to keep our five-year-old granddaughter occupied, Mimi gave our fifty-pound girl a piggyback ride. That was a bad choice. The next morning, I awoke with excruciating back pain. An MRI showed that innocent gesture had resulted in three bulging disks and one compression fracture. Moving, even getting out of bed, was difficult.

After my family returned home, I hurt badly, so the pain still impeded worship. I couldn't sit without pain, so I didn't attend Zoom meetings with my sisters or a Zoom Bible study I usually joined. Though in later attacks the Lord would tell me to worship through the pain, during this time, lying around was all I did. The next week, Wade injured his hip. We knew assaults were to derail us from our *higher* journey, so we did what we could to continue. About three weeks after my injury when I could again sit long enough to play the piano, I had another *higher* experience.

It was a Thursday. My back felt better than it had for days. Friday morning, I closed our bedroom window and twisted my back again. Intense pain was coupled with discouragement. I wanted to continue higher, but this injury would again hinder my journey. I endured pain that day and the next then went to bed propped up on pillows. When I awoke with a sharp throbbing at 1:00 a.m. on Sunday, I prayed a while, asking Holy Spirit to give direction for how to receive my healing. Suddenly, I felt oil on my fingertips, an indication that a miracle or a healing was in the making. I rubbed the oil over my lower back and touched Wade's head as he slept. I lay awake, praying for anyone I thought of who needed His touch. Then Holy Spirit led me to go to my office to pray.

THE ANSWER

With much effort, I got up, hobbled in, and painfully sat in my chair. My fingertips were still sticky with heavenly oil, so I rubbed them on my back again. I added anointing oil from the bottle beside my chair. I prayed in tongues for several minutes. As my heavenly language reached Father's ear, tears splashed down my face. I gingerly gathered those tears and also rubbed them on my back. Worshiping the Lord, I prayed and sang in tongues. Tangible power invaded the room. Finally, travail broke out as I felt Him doing a work in my body.

My hand vibrated, another indication of an imminent miracle. The Lord gave scriptures to stand on, including "The light of the eyes rejoiceth the heart: and a good report maketh the bones fat" (Prov. 15:30 KJV). I obeyed everything He impressed on me, including praying for fat bones in my back. I asked why healing had eluded me and what else I should do. Holy Spirit reminded me that God calls us by name, knows us intimately, and never sleeps nor grows weary in giving good things (see Isa. 40:26, 28). At all times, He has my back and pain on His mind.

That night He prompted me that my job is to make myself available, listen, obey, and use His ability and leading for the answer. No matter what He asks, I should do it faithfully. Every day, I should be ready whenever, wherever, and however He says. I emerged from my office an hour later, and standing didn't hurt. I slept the rest of the night without pain. The next morning and over the next few days I still ached; but I repeated, "My back is healed." I decided to obey what the Lord had said—whatever He led me to do.

Armed with a pillow, I gingerly walked from the car and into church that Sunday morning. In the foyer, I asked several prayer warriors if they would lay hands on my back during ministry at the end of service. Pain was intense during church; but as the altar later filled up, those people I'd asked came to where I was and laid hands on me. The following week, my back continued to hurt but was exponentially better. I didn't let words of negativity leave my mouth but rather thanked the Lord for my healing, despite the process not being complete.

The next Sunday, I brought my pillow again. A guest missionary's sermon on desperation spoke to my situation. When his preaching ended, he said those who were desperate should come and kneel at the altar. I answered that call and found a spot where I could push myself up later from my kneeling position. As I was crying out to God, my pastor's wife walked down from the worship team and laid her hands right where my back was hurting. Power surged from her hands into me. When I rose from the altar, I didn't need to push myself up. The work He began in my office that night was finished at the altar as Stacey obeyed Holy Spirit's leading. The next week and beyond, it felt wonderful. My pillow never went back with me to church.

A few months later I began to ache again in a different location. One morning during Sunday School, the Lord whispered to me to do a prophetic action. Before we dismissed, I asked our teacher, Dennis, if we could sing a chorus. That led several, including me, into travail. I tried to lay my head on the table in front of me as I cried, but I couldn't put it down all the way because of pain. I leaned against my elbows as my body reacted to sobs of travail in that breakthrough anointing. We'd been praying and crying for a few minutes when Dennis felt led to walk around the class and lay his hands on each of us. As he touched my head, anointing flowed through my body. Immediately, I could put my head all the way down on the table. I left Sunday school without pain. That's *higher*.

PART TWO

EZEKIEL'S JOURNEY

CHAPTER THREE
Ezekiel, the Glory

After being healed from the pain, Wade and I got back into the pattern of seeking *higher*, and we had more awesome glory encounters. I reflected on what the Lord had shown me, but I didn't understand everything. I was confused about the many faces I'd seen around the piano. Some looked human, but others resembled animals. I specifically saw a lion, and I couldn't understand why. Within a couple days, I had my explanation. One morning, God led me to begin my devotions in the book of "Ezekiel." I didn't know then, but the Lord wanted to let Ezekiel instruct me about *higher*. That research would be part of the glory series I'd teach later that spring. Studying so I could inform others about that subject helped my own understanding of what God wanted me to know about *higher*.

THE MAN

Ezekiel probably lived in Jerusalem before being taken captive by Nebuchadnezzar. As his book begins, he'd been exiled in Babylonia for five years among other captives at the River Chebar, a canal which could be navigated and fed into the Euphrates (see 1:2–3).[6] Chebar means "force or strength."[7] Euphrates means "that makes fruitful."[8] Both definitions would be significant traits for Ezekiel as he fulfilled what God would ask him to do. Holy Spirit is fire and strength which create fruitfulness. Through Him, we navigate our Christian journey.

At the beginning of his book, Ezekiel was probably thirty years old because that's when priests began ministries[9] (see Num. 4:3). Ezekiel and his dad Buzi were priests, likely from the family of Zadok,[10] one of David's priests (see 1 Chron. 16:39). Sons of Zadok drew near to the Lord to minister (see 40:46) while others usually attended to the people. That description fits with glory events Ezekiel describes as he drew closer to God in all ways. Although I'd read his book before, Ezekiel's experiences suddenly meant more in the light of my quest for *higher*. Beginning in Chapter One, his description of angels answered questions I'd been pondering.

MEETING THE LORD

While at Chebar, the heavens opened, and Ezekiel saw visions of God. Witnessing these visions distinguished Ezekiel from other prophets, for few have been allowed to see the LORD in His glory. Through open visions God gave him unique insight into His glory.[11] Though many visions are with our spiritual eyes rather than literally seeing an object or scene, an open vision operates as if we're there. In the first three chapters, Ezekiel has three open visions of God's glory (see 1:4; 3:12–13, 22–23). During this time, God likely spoke to him audibly.[12] These glory scenes announced His call to Ezekiel, a ministry that would last about twenty years.[13]

Many aspects of Ezekiel's experiences speak to me. First, "the word of Lord came expressly to Ezekiel" (1:3). The "word of the Lord" designates an important message from God. Words and callings from God are specifically for us though they're usually also to pass along to others. That wording may indicate his call wasn't simply a vague concept but a reality for Ezekiel.[14] Ezekiel's name itself is derived from a verb which means "to seize, to hold fast" which indicates "he was a man whom God had seized."[15] The Lord seized Ezekiel and wouldn't let him go until he heard God's message. Has the Lord ever apprehended you like He grasped Ezekiel, Moses, Jonah, Noah, Saul/Paul, and others? He chose them for a purpose and wouldn't let them go.

Then, "the hand of the Lord was upon him there" (see 1:3). The "hand of the Lord" denotes that Holy Spirit arrived for revelation.[16] For a difficult job, His hand strengthens and enables His prophets so they'll avoid operating from their own will rather than God's.[17] It indicates His power and might and signifies He'll always be with His people. His hand helps, empowers, and disciplines His kids, yet it's deadly to enemies.[18] How appropriate that from the beginning, God's hand influenced Ezekiel! We all should follow the leading and power His hand brings.

Ezekiel probably hadn't processed what had happened when he saw a whirlwind and huge cloud with a great fire engulfing itself.[19] Fire is a glory manifestation. Years ago in one of our services, God's glory descended profusely. The room's southwest side was uncomfortably hot. Pictures taken during that time showed an incredible sight. A face emerged in the window and then revealed fire coming from His mouth. The glory had visited us with this fiery event. Ezekiel described his visions of God as a "raging fire . . . [with] brightness all around" (Ezek. 1:4), which surrounded the flames and radiated outward in an amber color (see 1:4).

FACES

From the fiery cloud, Ezekiel saw the likeness of four living creatures (see 1:5). The number four symbolizes completeness.[20] His living creatures' appearances had completeness all around. With four faces, they looked different directions because God sees everywhere.[21] Each face was unique—a man in front, lion on the right, ox on the left, and eagle in the back (see 1:10–11). Ezekiel's description astounded me. I'd been confused about the animal faces in my pictures from our worship. Those had been angels, living creatures, like Ezekiel had seen.

The variety of faces showed different animals over whom God rules: humanity, beasts of the field (wild or domestic), and birds of the air. Four faces could have signified the world's four corners. God's representatives, both human and angelic, cover the earth to accomplish His instructions.[22] Later, the Lord would allude to earth as He gave a word to Ezekiel about how an end had come to the "four corners of the land" (7:2). In Revelation John also spoke of four angels at the earth's four corners holding four winds. He saw another angel announcing God's judgment and carrying God's seal with instructions to the angels (see Rev. 7:1–2). I applied the meanings of the number four to the angel touching my fourth toe. Like Aaron and his sons needed to consecrate themselves, my actions must also be holy and acceptable to God.

The animals' faces may show that no matter the species, God rules over all and that everything was made to worship Him, but these four are elevated within their species.[23] A lion represents courage, majesty, and might (see 2 Sam. 17:10; Prov. 28:1). An eagle embodies swiftness and far-seeing wisdom as it "mount[s] up at [God's] command, and make[s] its nest on high" (Job 39:27). Its eyes scrutinize long distances to spy out prey. An ox or bull denotes power, strength, and much harvest: "Where no oxen are, the trough is clean; but much increase comes by the strength of an ox" (see Prov. 14:4). Where work and productivity occur, a variety of messes will inevitably transpire. Instead of indicating what we're doing wrong, those predicaments suggest results. Finally, man, created in God's image, has intelligence and dominion in the earth. As living creatures' faces included all these animals, so should their characteristics apply to God's other beings, including humans. We should be elevated to work effectively for God's Kingdom. Looking from His perspective, we can conquer the enemy. We should be courageous, wise, strong, and fruitful. The Lord was saying I should cultivate these traits to progress higher.

The living creatures sparkled like bronze, had four wings, and possessed straight legs. Their soles were like calves' feet, and a man's hands were under the wings on four sides (see 1:7–8). Our hands are to be raised consistently in praise to God (also in 10:8). Each living creature's wings touched each other. Two wings brushed against one another, and two covered their bodies probably to show reverence to God's presence.[24] Living creatures had an appearance of burning coals, similar to torches going back and forth like flashes of lightning (see 1:11, 13–14).

WHEEL-IN-A-WHEEL

On the ground beside each living creature were wheels high and awesome. *Awesome* is *yirah*, meaning "reverence ... fear"[25] (see 1:15–18). The wheels' immense height may represent God's greatness and wisdom.[26] Ezekiel's revelations often stressed respect for the Lord. Those wheels could also signify the connection from heaven to earth in this world and the next.[27] The writer of Romans says, "Oh, the depth of the riches both of the wisdom and knowledge of God!" (Rom. 11:33). How can we fathom the Lord's ways or the depth our Christian walk can reach unless we explore *higher*?

All four creatures had a second wheel in the middle of the outer wheels (see 1:16). The meaning of a wheel-in-a-wheel symbol could have many possibilities. These wheels may have been multiple angelic orbs. Wheels could represent time's progression because everything moves and doesn't remain motionless.[28] Perhaps the living creatures' wings symbolized the heavens, but the wheels were planted on earth. Maybe this construction showed how the Trinity resides in us, and we reside in Them. The wheels' positioning at right angles allowed them to go in any direction,[29] so maybe this shows how the Spirit can lead us anywhere. On temple carts, ten bases were described similarly to the living creatures with lions, oxen, and cherubim on panels between frames and wheels at the four corners (see 1 Ki. 7:29–30).[30]

The wheels' rims had eyes all around. This great number of eyes may symbolize God's vast awareness because the "eyes of Lord . . . scan to and fro throughout the whole earth" (Zech. 4:10). Eyes everywhere may speak of His all-seeing nature and supreme intelligence[31] or represent His being in all places or able to see and move in every direction.[32] Man is made in God's likeness, so perhaps eyes represent how we should look from God's perspective, like the eagle.

By extension, the wheels raised and moved beside the living creatures. They went up when the creatures were lifted because "the spirit of living creatures was in the wheels" (see 1:20). When living creatures moved, stood, or lifted, wheels responded to the living creature's spirit. *Spirit* is *ruwach*, meaning "spirit, wind, and breath." That word is used often in the first three chapters of Ezekiel. It's translated as *spirit* whether "the human spirit, distressing spirit, or Spirit of God."[33] Holy Spirit is part of our being; He's inside us and a factor in all we do including where, when, and how we advance. We shouldn't turn aside from where He sends us. Just as God had directed and would guide Ezekiel, their spirit led the living creatures. All went forward wherever their spirit wanted to go and didn't turn from their course (see 1:12). When Holy Spirit speaks to our spirits, we must go where He says, do what He wants, and not deviate until He sends us another direction. God doesn't make mistakes. He has plans for us; to stray from them would be rebellion.

TRANSLATIONS

I love the wheels being "lifted" (1:20). *Lifted* is *nasa*, to "arise . . . carry (away) . . . raise up . . . take (away, up)."[34] The miracle of supernatural travel from one place to another is called translations or transportations. In addition to translations that occurred at the time of his calling and commission, Ezekiel would experience others. For example, he was later transported from his place of exile back to the gate at Jerusalem's temple (see 8:3).

Ezekiel wasn't the only biblical person who experienced a translation. Jesus vanished, Paul was caught up in Paradise (second Heaven), and Philip was carried to Azotus (see Lk. 24:31; 2 Cor. 12:2–4; Acts 8:39). Elijah understood and put translations into practice. I love when Obadiah balked at the prophet's request to bring Ahab to him so they could talk. Obadiah, Ahab's servant, feared that when he returned, Elijah may have flown elsewhere. If so, Ahab would kill Obadiah. Elijah assured him he'd be there (see 1 Ki. 18:7–15). That tells me Elijah understood how to be translated on purpose! Now, that's taking the limits off God.

I'd never experienced my body's translation until my quest for *higher*:

> One night during worship, for a few seconds I was transported from my living room and was walking on a country road. Beside me, a chain-link fence about my height encircled an area similar to a baseball field or horse arena. A roll comparable to a sleeping bag lay on the rail at the fence top. It stretched around the enclosed space as far as I could see. The vision was in black and white, but the roll was bright yellow.

As I watched this scene, I realized I was somewhere other than my living room. I snapped out of that location and back to my house. I'm not sure why I experienced that particular scene or its significance, but I believe it was a physical translation. That's *higher*! Though I'm not sure why I was there, I got a message. Two meanings of yellow are "faith and glory of God."[35] Both relate to a higher walk where amazing glory events occur, but faith is necessary to believe and receive. The yellow might also have been referencing the color of beryl that was around the wheels and workings that moved by and with the Spirit.

Later, I dreamed orbs lifted me to fly around during a class we were teaching. Shortly after that, two different people geographically far apart had similar dreams about flying. Another message could parallel Jesus' meaning when He was reaching toward me from the top of the riser. To go higher, I had to get into God's glory. No opening existed around the arena in my vision; to access it, I would need a glory event. I believe we will experience that phenomenon again, but it won't be by our might. Translations are real and part of a higher walk.

SOUND

Ezekiel saw the awesome, crystal-colored firmament of Heaven above the living creatures (see 1:22). He also experienced an aspect of God's ability that most people never perceive—God's amazing voice. Under the firmament, two wings which covered each living creature's side spread toward each other. Ezekiel later compared the loud sound of cherubim's wings to the Almighty's voice (see 1:23–24; 10:5; 43:2). John reiterated that God's voice resembled the "voice of many waters" (Rev. 14:2). I can imagine the overwhelming clamor as John "heard the voice of many angels around the throne, the living creatures, and the elders . . . . Their number was ten thousand times ten thousand, and thousands of thousands" (Rev. 5:11). The noise of that magnitude of living creatures must have echoed around that island as John received his revelations.

The same was true of Ezekiel. He heard a tumult which erupted similarly to an army's noise. *Tumult* is *qowl*. A *qowl* can be loud or quiet. As a gentle sound, it means "to call aloud; voice or sound . . . bleating." As a boisterous reverberation, it means "proclamation . . . thunder (-ing), voice, + yell."[36] *Qowl* was that quiet voice that spoke to Elijah on the mountain (see 1 Ki. 19:12) but also that thundering trumpet sound as Israel shouted, and Jericho's walls collapsed (see Josh. 6:20). I heard a speaker say that when he was a new Christian, the Lord always spoke to him with a trumpet voice. Now, he's a more mature believer with greater sensitivity to God, so the Lord usually speaks in a whisper. A *qowl* speaks as God wills.

The ice-storm story about my family was a quiet but authoritative *qowl* spoken into my mother's spirit. Another childhood event demonstrated God speaking in a loud *qowl*. One brisk, autumn day, when I was an infant, Mom dressed my older sisters in warm attire to play outside. As they opened the kitchen door, a thunderous *qowl* boomed, "Stay in there!"

All of them, including Mom, were taken aback. She left us kids inside and investigated. No human was around, just God's mighty voice. She later learned that hunting season had begun that day. Because we lived beside a woods, a stray bullet could have been a real possibility. We never knew how that thunderous *qowl* saved them; but when the Lord speaks in a roar, obedience is crucial. God's no-nonsense *qowl* probably determined life or death for our young family as He'd again alerted my mother to the enemy's intentions.

The voice (*qowl*) Ezekiel heard came from the firmament above their heads. Living creatures stood, wings-down and immobile. That was probably both to respect and to hear clearly what God would say (see 1:24–25). Even angels let down their wings and stand in respect at His voice. As we stand still, Father can speak to us. His voice and presence require lowliness, humility, reverence, silence, and attention to hear Him. At those sacred times, we should "be still, and know that [He is] God" (Ps. 46:10) for the same reason as Jehoshaphat when he was in combat—"stand still and see the salvation of the Lord" (2 Chron. 20:17). When we remain still, we can receive a victorious battle plan. As we listen, we can reflect on His majesty, power, and revelations.

FATHER

Above the firmament, a throne was heavenly blue like sapphire (see 1:26). While angels moved to do His bidding, God's throne was stationary in the firmament because with the Lord, "no variation or shadow of turning" exists (Jas. 1:17). That expanse separated the living creatures from God.[37] One who appeared as a Man was high above, but Ezekiel didn't identify Him by name (see 1:26). That's likely because Hebrews treated God's name with such reverence they didn't speak it aloud.[38] Some say this Man was God in His glory while others say this was His Son. Whether Father or Son, an incredible encounter occurred.

From His waist up, amber-colored fire was all around. From the waist down, fire burned with brightness everywhere (see 1:27). In a later chapter, Ezekiel again described God as having fire from the waist down and brightness from the waist up (see 8:2). When Daniel described the Ancient of Days, he noted His throne and bottom wheels were also burning fire (see Dan. 7:9). John also experienced God's glory in a vision of an angel clothed in a cloud with a rainbow on his head, a face like the sun, and feet like pillars of fire (see Rev. 10:1–3).

Ezekiel saw the Lord's brightness, appearing as "a rainbow in a cloud on a rainy day" (1:28). God's glory can show up as fire but also as a beautiful rainbow. How appropriate that God used a rainbow to reassure Ezekiel of His majesty, power, promise, and mercy.[39] A rainbow brings hope on a stormy day, often while rain is still pouring. Though God's judgment may be a consuming fire, the rainbow reminds us of His covenant of love with His people.[40] After God's judgment a rainbow symbolized His mercy and forgiveness. Ezekiel's message to Israel would be the same. He was to convey a lesson of judgment and a promise of restoration.[41]

A weighty presence accompanied the glory. *Glory* is *kabod*, "weight, but only fig[uratively] in a good sense, splendor or copiousness."[42] Weightiness settles in with the glory like a heavy blanket. As we sit in His presence, we're rejuvenated. Resting in that *kabod* is referred to as "soaking" in His presence. The *kabod* comes for many reasons which I will mention later.

Exodus shows that His presence came for great revelation, demonstration, and protection (see Exod. 24:16–17; 33:18–19, 22). He comes to foster relationship, often as a result of worship. As a matter of fact, over the years, Holy Spirit has given me several dreams about a bath and soaking to say I've neglected my worship time. In each dream the message was the same: Don't overlook the time when the *kabod* gives renewed purpose, direction, peace, and strength.

Now, Ezekiel fell on his face when he heard God's voice (see 1:28). Several other times in his book, he fell face-down, likely because of the glory.[43] Being slain in the Spirit often accompanies God's presence (see Ezek. 1:28; Dan. 10:9, for example). However his falling could have also been about reverencing and adoring the Lord as angels had done. Showing respect to God is part of a Christian's purpose. When John encountered Jesus during his experience in "Revelation," he fell at His feet like he was dead (see Rev. 1:17). We should respect manifestations of His glory because that time is an amazing, precious experience. Those who dwell in and revere His presence are visited and directed by Him.

CHAPTER FOUR

Angels

Angels played a role in Ezekiel's calling. Many biblical references reveal angels' traits. They're common and abundant. Angels don't marry and may not appear in a recognizable form (see Matt. 22:30; Ezek. 40:3). They often interact with humans, so we should beware of how we treat others because we may be "unwittingly entertain[ing] angels" (Heb. 13:2). In God's hierarchy, man is considered slightly lower than angels, yet angels are amazed at our salvation (see Heb. 2:7; 1 Pet. 1:12). Despite their higher status, an angel's duty is to help man. They're "ministering spirits sent forth to minister for those who will inherit salvation" (Heb. 1:14). That's you and I.

God's given His angels the responsibility to guard and protect us—from evil, plagues, even stones we could trip on (see Ps. 91:9-12). Angels don't visit us on their own, but rather God sends them forth to accomplish specific purposes—to do whatever God asks. David said, "Bless the Lord, you His angels, who excel in strength, who do His word, heeding the voice of His word. Bless the Lord, all you His hosts, you ministers of His, who do His pleasure" (Ps. 103:20-21). An angel informed Zacharias about the impending birth of his son John; an angel visited Gethsemane to strengthen Jesus before His crucifixion (see Lk. 1:11-13; 22:43). They were present as He ascended to Heaven after His resurrection, and they clarified to witnesses about Jesus' return (see Acts 1:11). An Angel of the Lord accompanied Moses on Mount Sinai, and an angel told Paul that the men on the ship would be saved despite the great storm (see Acts 7:38; 27:23-24).

John's visions show multiple examples of angelic roles. The number of angels he saw in the end-time army was 200 million (see Rev. 9:16). Whether that's a literal figure or a symbol representing a profuse number, an abundance of angels exists. Jesus also indicated numerous angels when

He told persecutors and executioners that if He chose to do so, He could call twelve legions of angels to free Him (see Matt. 26:53). That number would be 6,000 at His immediate call.[44] Angels will come with Jesus at His return to give rewards according to works. They'll separate the wicked from the just (see Matt. 16:27; 13:49), preach the gospel, bring instructions, and give the key to the bottomless pit. They'll stand at the altar before God, fill censers with fire from the altar, and then throw them to earth (see Rev. 14:6–7; 9:1; 8:2–7). More biblical examples of angels demonstrate their crucial roles in past, present, and end times.

THEIR PRESENCE

Angelic activity accompanies the glory as they interact with us. Arms may tingle, or we may experience other signs, including hearing or smelling them. You might see them with spiritual or natural eyes. I've observed angels often with my spiritual eye, but a few times I've detected them in the natural. During our Times of Refreshing services, many have felt angelic presences during worship, and that heavenly atmosphere stayed for the whole service. While leaving the building, I glanced at the roof. With my natural eye, I once saw one angel. Another night two were flying around, dancing before Father with the sacrifice of worship we'd brought to Him.

When angels arrive, they often usher in the glory. Seeing or even sensing angelic presences is incredible, so being excited is normal, but angels and other signs and wonders shouldn't be the main focus of our journey. Glory manifestations and angelic presences aren't the reason we should rejoice—He is. We don't exalt anything else besides God (see Col. 2:18). For them and us, His presence is the reason for our adulation. Though angels have other assignments, their main job is to worship the Lord. It should be ours, too, because it's all about Him, and He is worthy.

PROTECTION

A major assignment angels fulfill is protection. When disciples wanted children not to bother Jesus, He told them not to despise "little ones [because] their angels always see the face of [the] Father" (Matt. 18:10). Because the word *their* is possessive, Jesus was indicating that even children have angels specifically assigned to them. Our personal heavenly companions watch over us and our loved ones because the "angel of the Lord encamps all around those who fear Him, and delivers them" (Ps. 34:7). The Lord gives angels responsibility for our safety. I've experienced that promise many times. After I've called upon God for supernatural protection, He's answered by sending angels.

Once, I was to speak at a ladies' conference in Savannah, Georgia, a more-than-700-mile trip. As we merged onto I-75 in Northern Kentucky, I noticed what I would see often during that trip. In my peripheral vision, several white objects flitted around. I thought my eyes were doing something weird, so I made a mental note to tell my optometrist at my next appointment. Those white flashes occurred other times during the drive and in our hotel room that weekend. I didn't understand the significance until we started home Sunday afternoon.

Wade was tired; so unlike his normal practice, he asked me to drive a while so he could nap. Singing to pass the time, I traveled slightly over the speed limit on that crowded interstate which was under construction. When I lowered my window for fresh air and passed concrete barriers, a flapping sound echoed. I knew our tires were making the noise, so I slowed down in that fast-moving traffic and eased over to the far-right lane. I woke Wade and told him what I'd heard. As he filled the tires with air at the next exit, he discovered a huge lump on one tire.

We stayed in that town until the next day when businesses opened. A man at a tire shop said we could've easily been killed if pressure had pushed on that weak spot. God had saved us by sending angels to put their hands on that tire and protect us on our Kingdom mission. The Lord doesn't give aid to angels but "gives aid to the seed of Abraham" (Heb. 2:16). That includes us, and that promise is fulfilled through angels. My family and I are living testimonies of that. More than once, angels have steered my car to safety in traffic when an accident was inevitable.

My sister, Anita, had a similar experience. She was driving in the interstate's fast lane when her front tire blew out. Though traffic was moving quickly, she managed to cross two crowded lanes and ease onto the shoulder. When her husband arrived and investigated, he found marks on the bumper where her car had actually skidded on the pavement. She shouldn't have been able to maneuver all the way over and park on the shoulder, but she did. However what was inside her car told the story—massive, white dust. She initially assumed the covering was from an air bag but was later assured it wasn't. A mechanic told her husband he didn't "know how she kept the vehicle on the road." God had again protected one of His children with heavenly emissaries to steer her vehicle to safety. Angels have an assignment—us!

JACK

Another time, the Lord's protection through angels saved a young boy. While my friend Evelyn was teaching Sunday School, she took her class out to play. Tag was the first activity she thought of with that energetic group, which included her eight-year-old son Jack. They'd been running a while when he tried to escape a classmate's pursuit. Darting between two parked cars, he scurried into the path of an automobile entering the parking lot. Evelyn's heart dropped as a thud alerted her that he'd been hit.

"Jack!" she screamed.

Immediately he responded. "I'm under the car, and I'm alive." He'd been hit from the front and dragged between the back wheels. Seeing his foot twisted beneath the tire, Evelyn was certain it was broken, but her main realization was that the other tire stopped barely an inch from his head.

Paramedics arrived, loaded him into the ambulance, and allowed Evelyn to ride in the front to the hospital. From behind her, Jack's voice echoed as he talked to the paramedic.

"I'm okay! I saw God's angel wrap his arms around me to protect me from that car."

Astonished by her son's words, Evelyn was speechless. The Father she'd grown to love had fulfilled His promise—He'd cradled Jack in "the cleft of the rock, and . . . cover[ed him] with [His] hand" (Exod. 33:22). That was the angel's assignment—to protect God's precious Jack. Her tears flowed as concern changed to rejoicing. The hospital observed him overnight; but except for minor road rash, he was fine. The Great Shepherd had sent His angels because He loved Jack and his mother so very much. He holds us and our kids in His arms of protection. Even beneath a car.

Isaiah gave a synopsis of the role of angels: "When you pass through the waters, I will be with you; and through the rivers, they shall not overflow you. When you walk through the fire, you shall not be burned, nor shall the flame scorch you" (Isa. 43:2). God covered Evelyn's son as He shielded him from injury or worse. We won't be overwhelmed nor destroyed because the Lord sends emissaries to protect us from fire, rushing rivers, or the impact of an oncoming car.

COMFORT

Angels often come to comfort. My husband and I had been at his parents' farm the night his dad passed away. I went home before him, grieving the loss of a man I dearly loved but with whom I'd spent far too few days. I parked in the garage behind our house, wearily shuffled up the sidewalk, and turned the knob at back door. As I opened it, I felt a strong angelic manifestation. Along with the tingly feeling of their presence, an unfamiliar, sweet, floral odor engulfed me. It was so strong that for a moment I was frightened, thinking someone was in the room with me. As I realized angels had come to console me, my fear turned to rejoicing. "You, O Lord, are a shield for me, my glory and the One who lifts up my head" (Ps. 3:3). He shields and comforts. When Wade came home and I shared the experience, both of us were consoled by the presence of His angels.

Several years later and during my higher journey, angels again showed up to bring comfort. A friend diagnosed with Alzheimer's had been put into a psychiatric hospital for a brief evaluation. She was combative and frightened by her new environment, so her husband called to calm her. She told him she couldn't talk right then because Connie was with her. Her husband later called me to ask why the hospital had let me in to see her but told him to wait until visiting days. When I assured him that I had been at home, nearly three hours away, we both rejoiced. God had sent an angel to comfort my friend, and the heavenly emissary was in the form of someone with whom she was familiar and comfortable. If God could send her an angel for comfort, He could certainly heal her terrible disease. I'm still standing on that promise.

DREAMS

Sometimes protection comes as the result of a dream. If we pray to avoid what Father warned us about, we may never know what the outcome might have been. Biblical examples demonstrate God's protection through dreams—Joseph, for example. God entrusted His Son's well-being to His earthly father via dreams. An angel told Joseph through a dream to take Mary as his wife, to flee from Herod and go to Egypt, and to return to Israel after Herod's death (see Matt. 1:20; 2:13, 19). Wise men were "divinely warned" in a dream not to go back to Herod (Matt. 2:12). I believe that divine warning was delivered by angels who were watching out for their Boss' Child.

Dreams have alerted my family to snares that lay ahead. Once, my sister, who was a prison guard, dreamed she was killed after being taken hostage. She awoke when God's audible voice said, "You are Christ's, and Christ is God's" (1 Cor. 3:23). About two years later, another sister dreamed about a knife to our sister's throat. Our family intensely prayed. A few days later, as my sister did her prison inventory, Holy Spirit led her to pray again. About an hour later, two inmates came from behind a door and held shanks to the throats of my sister and another staff member. Thirty-four other prisoners could have joined the attack, but they didn't. Holy Spirit gave peace that passes all understanding (see Phil. 4:7), so my sister was able to negotiate. Because Holy Spirit had come before to warn of impending danger, the hostage situation lasted only about a half hour, and everyone emerged uninjured. As a bonus, my sister and the other staff member received the highest Medal of Honor for their actions during the crisis.

Another incredible *higher* experience occurred as I've written this book. Before I left for a trip to the Southwest, a simple dream bothered me. I saw a brown spider with long legs perched on a wall. Though that was brief, I couldn't get it off my mind. I asked my daughter in Oklahoma to anoint and pray over their house and family because brown recluses had been inside their home before. Wade and I also prayed that if the spider represented a spiritual attack, the Lord would protect us. I covered potential meanings with prayer, but my spirit was still disturbed by the simple dream. I knew Holy Spirit wanted me to act on it further.

I traveled to Arizona a couple weeks after the dream and stayed with Anita. I'd planned to ask what kind of spider resembled the one in my dream, but the answer revealed itself before I could. As she walked through her dining room, she spotted a spider on the wall. It was the one I had dreamed about—the same size, color, and body structure. Because Anita hadn't seen that type before, she looked for a picture of a brown recluse. It was identical. We later spotted several more in her guest bath. Through a dream, God had warned and protected us from potential danger. Dreams the angels bring are great weapons in our Holy Spirit arsenal.

PART TWO | EZEKIEL'S JOURNEY

LIVING CREATURES, CHERUBIM, AND SERAPHIM

Cherubim

Through many biblical examples, we can learn much about different types of angels. In Chapter One, Ezekiel described living creatures in great detail. They had features in common with both seraphim and cherubim. Though he called them living creatures in earlier chapters, he later said they were cherubim (see 10:15, for example). Perhaps when he first saw them, he knew little about the glory realm. As he experienced more events, he moved beyond what he and others knew about God and the heavenly domain. In a later chapter, he said cherubim lifted their wings and wheels while God's glory (*kabod*) lingered high above on a mountain (see 11:23).

In his vision, the apostle John also depicted angels as living creatures and described their faces as Ezekiel had: a lion, calf, eagle, and man (see Rev. 4:7). However, these angels in John's vision may have been seraphim because they had six wings. He said, "They do not rest day or night, saying: 'Holy, holy, holy, Lord God Almighty, Who was and is and is to come!'" (Rev. 4:8). To declare that He is holy is appropriate for us too. For Hebrews everything about worship was considered holy—garments, anointing oil, and even the table and utensils (Exod. 28:3; 30:25, 27). When they gave adoration to Father, like Ezekiel, elders fell reverently before God and worshiped. Cherubim are usually beside or around God's throne.[45] Because of this, they're often called "throne angels."[46] Their job of worshiping and guarding the throne is continual.

Cherubim serve in God's presence and implement His orders. Like Ezekiel's description of living creatures, cherubim have four faces and wings. They're associated with God's holiness and glory and guard God's holy domain from sin and immorality.[47] The Bible describes them in several places. The Psalmist said when God delivered him from trouble, the Lord traveled on a cherub "and flew upon the wings of the wind" (see Ps. 18:10). Cherubim were at the Garden of Eden's east entrance with a flaming sword, turning each way to guard the path to the tree of life (see Gen. 3:24). Two golden cherubim adorned the ends of the Ark of the Covenant with their wings spread upward to cover and protect the Ark. They faced each another and looked toward the mercy seat (see Exod. 25:18–20).[48] Cherubim are often beside us as we worship.

Seraphim

Because Seraphim are so close to God, they're considered the highest rank of angels.[49] They fly above His throne with a primary duty to glorify and praise Him continuously. I believe that when they see Father, they're compelled to worship because of utter love for Him. In Isaiah, the voice of the seraph was so powerful that doorposts shook, and smoke filled the house (see Isa. 6:1–4). As a result of their duties, and likely because of the smoke that accompanies their worship, seraphim are sometimes called "Burning Ones"[50] or nobles. Like these angels, our job is to praise the Lord continually (see Ps. 34:1).

Seraphim may be God's personal attendants. They have six wings: two are for flying; two cover their feet; and two conceal their face. The wings which envelop their feet (see Isa. 6:2) likely demonstrate their humility. Feet were believed to be unclean and unworthy to show God. That act of covering their faces may demonstrate reverence because God's full glory is too powerful to behold. Ezekiel displayed his meekness as he bowed or fell down in God's presence. The gift of coming into His presence is truly humbling.

Seraphim played a role in Isaiah's prophetic commissioning. As he saw a vision of God on His throne, seraphim flew above it. After his confession about having "unclean lips" (Isa. 6:5), a seraph flew over him and with a coal from the altar touched his lips and declared him free from sin (see Isa. 6:5–7). Isaiah received his commission after seeing a revelation of the Lord, confessing his sin, and allowing God to cleanse. Humility in recognizing then correcting faults draws Him to us. After this, Isaiah was purified and qualified to be God's prophet. For a seraph to have such a major role in a human's sanctification says much about their status. Isaiah heard an angel cry out to another, saying, "Holy, holy, holy is the Lord of hosts; the whole earth is full of His glory!" (Isa. 6:3). The seraphim's song has also been sung by Christians as praise to Father.[51]

John described seraphim as he gave details about living creatures. He said they "were full of eyes all around and within" (Rev. 4:8). This is different from Ezekiel's initial vision because he described eyes all around on the wheels. In a later chapter, he mentioned not only wheels but also angels as being covered with eyes (see 10:12). Because their job is to worship God constantly and not rest day or night, maybe the abundance of eyes allows angels to be always alert. Perhaps those eyes are necessary as they worship because no matter how they look at the Lord, He's worthy of constant adulation. The differences between the seraphim's and living creatures' songs mentioned by John and Isaiah seem insignificant. However, the seraphim focus on God's glory, while the living creatures declare who God is. Angels have much to teach us.

CHAPTER FIVE
Ezekiel, the Call and Preparation

Chapter Two begins when God told Ezekiel to stand, and He would speak to him (see 2:1). God called him, "Son of man" (2:3). This name was used ninety plus times about Ezekiel, once with Daniel, but wasn't used to describe any other prophet until Jesus Christ, Who was called this because He came to a fallen world as a man (see Lk. 19:10).[52] Ezekiel was a man whose job was to go to a fallen nation. Perhaps God used that name to keep him humble rather than allow him to be exalted by his wealth of revelations and glory experiences.[53]

Right before Chapter Two, Ezekiel had fallen in reverence to God. How amazing that when you consider yourself nothing special, He can use you mightily. We should "humble [ourselves] under the mighty hand of God, that He may exalt [us] in due time" (1 Pet. 5:6). Peter demonstrated this. After the celebrated healing at the Gate Beautiful, people marveled at Peter and John's giftings, but Peter didn't let pride creep in at others' acknowledgement. He refused to take credit for what God had done. He said, "Why do you marvel at this? Or why look so intently at us, as though by our own power or godliness we had made this man walk?" (Acts. 3:12). To paraphrase, "Don't look at me! I didn't do it." What God does through us or allows us to be part of correlates with our obedience and availability. It's His ability and our availability. Practicing meekness like Peter and Ezekiel allows God to exalt us.

HOLY SPIRIT

Holy Spirit entered Ezekiel and set him on his feet as God spoke (see 2:2). Ezekiel's experience was special. In the Old Testament, Holy Spirit was *upon*, not *in* people. Later, Ezekiel would prophesy about Holy Spirit coming to live inside us (see 36:27). He understood that concept because his glory experiences resembled Holy Spirit's activity in the New Testament and today. On the Day of Pentecost, Holy Spirit engulfed people, and they were filled with the Spirit (see Acts 2:1–4). Like He demonstrated magnificent signs and wonders to and through those filled with the Spirit after Acts 2, Ezekiel personally experienced many startling wonders that Holy Spirit fashioned long before the New Testament event.

The Old Testament occurrence of indwelling this prophet isn't surprising. Ezekiel is considered the charismatic prophet. His writings are sometimes referred to as "acts of Holy Spirit in the Old Testament."[54] Perhaps God showed up in a mighty way to encourage Ezekiel because from the beginning of his journey, the Lord had told him that he'd see little success in changing the rebellious behaviors. Though he'd seemingly fail at his job of speaking to backslidden Israel, Ezekiel still obeyed. However, Israel's denying this message was from the Lord would be impossible because of signs and wonders which occurred (see 2:5).

HEAR AND OBEY

Later, Holy Spirit lifted Ezekiel by his hair (see 8:3). Now, God spoke aloud, and Ezekiel "heard Him who spoke" (2:2). *Heard* is *shama*, "to hear intelligently (often with impl[ication] of attention, obedience, etc.)"[55] When God speaks, the hearer has a choice about if or how he or she wants to hear then obey. From this first exchange, Ezekiel listened like we should—with attention and obedience. Ezekiel's ministry started with submission to do what was outside his comfort zone. However having Holy Spirit dwell inside him was a tremendous help.

Many biblical saints demonstrated dynamics of hearing with attention and obedience. Philip, for example, had been the featured speaker at a dynamic Samaritan revival which impacted multitudes. God sent an angel to tell him to go to a desert place in Gaza and minister to only one. He didn't consider himself too prominent as a preacher to do such an insignificant task. He obeyed and ran to do so (see Acts 8:5–8, 26–27). As a result, he experienced a glory event, a translation, like Ezekiel did repeatedly. We never know what compliance to God's directives will accomplish.

Recently, a man at church asked if I recalled a word I'd given him six or seven years before. Going through a divorce, he felt his world had fallen apart. He was a minister who loved God, but he'd descended so low he thought his only answer was to "check out." After he declared that to himself, he went to church one Sunday morning where Holy Spirit gave me a word of knowledge. As soon as ministry time arrived, I hustled to where he was sitting and told him that God had a word for him. He just looked at me, ready to hear, but not hopeful. His feeling of having nowhere to go right then had given him a sense of overwhelming futility.

"God said to tell you not to 'check out.'" I usually don't say that phrase, but I've learned to repeat what God says and how He says it. I might attempt to make His revelation clearer using my limited understanding, but He doesn't need my help. That man was confused but amazed. How did I know those words he'd spoken privately to the Lord? God had revealed his frame of mind, heard his pronouncement, and even knew his thoughts. He decided that despite what his life looked like at the time, he was going to respond and check back in. Now, he has a wonderful wife who was God's perfect choice for him, and the Lord has led them into ever-expanding ministry. God's word changes lives, and our obedience can make a difference to someone's destiny. Ezekiel heard what God asked him to do and listened with an attitude of obedience.

THE REBELLIOUS

Father told Ezekiel he'd be going to His rebellious nation with impudent and stubborn people. God warned him that he'd encounter hardships and rebellious attitudes as he fulfilled his calling, but the Lord also brought encouragement. Whether His people heard, obeyed, or refused, they'd recognize Ezekiel as a prophet (see 2:3–6). When God sends us, we proceed in His authority and power. That concept reminds me of one of my favorite scriptures: "A man's gift makes room for him, and brings him before great men" (Prov. 18:16). If we're attacked because of our anointing or those who are rebellious don't heed our words, God proves our callings when our giftings and His words through us come to pass. He stressed that concept to Ezekiel and reiterated the idea in later chapters. Like God reassured Ezekiel in Chapter Two, He again said that after prophetic words prove themselves, "they will know that a prophet has been among them" (Ezek. 33:33).

Though Israel had transgressed against God, He loved His rebellious children enough to send messages through Ezekiel and others. God didn't call them the house of Israel, but now the house of rebellion. "Rebellious nation" is the same wording used in the Old Testament to refer to Gentiles.[56] Elijah encountered these dynamics with a rebellious Israel. He'd faced Jezebel, Ahab, and later their son Ahaziah's anger and persecution for speaking God's words. They'd attempted to kill him multiple times. On Mt. Carmel, the whole nation stood against him. God, however, proved Elijah's gifts as fire lapped up the sacrifice and more. As a result, the nation turned back to God en masse (see 1 Ki. 18:21, 39; 19:1–2; 2 Ki. 1:10–11). Additionally, during and as a result of his persecutions, God brought promotion for Elijah. His prophecies not only came to pass, but Elijah's Holy Spirit abilities were also expanded.

God told Ezekiel three times not to be afraid or dismayed by the rebellious, their words, or their looks (see 2:6). He should be aware of *briers* (which means "rebels") and *thorns* (which is a Hebrew root, meaning "to sting"). Both describe the wicked.[57] The Aramaic root for *thorns* means "to contradict."[58] Some would not only ignore him, but they'd contradict his words. God showed people's potential for cruelty to Ezekiel and his potential response. These warnings would prepare Ezekiel to expect his own adverse reactions that could deter him from relaying God's message. Regardless of acceptance or rejection, he should still speak God's words. And he did.

Even when God gives a hard word, we must convey it. We join the rebellious ranks if we neglect to share His words. How could Ezekiel speak God's warnings to the disobedient if he didn't obey? Jonah reaped rebellion's penalties when he rejected his assignment to Ninevah, a people he hated but God loved (see Jon. 1:17). Jesus came to those He loved but who rejected Him and His words of love and reproof (see Matt. 13:53–58). God repeated Ezekiel's assignment multiple times (see Ezek. 2:4, 7, for example). When He asks us to commit to an appointment that will have a cost, His instructions are clear, though specifics will become apparent as we proceed.

PREPARATION

In Chapter Two, the Lord delineates Ezekiel's calling, but the prophet needed more instruction before he received his commission. Although Father gives a call to many, only a few are chosen (see Matt. 22:14). The Greek word for *called* is *kletos*, meaning to be "invited."[59] *Chosen* is *eklektos*, meaning "select; by impli[cation] favorite ... elect."[60] One meaning of being "chosen" is to have "met all the [necessary] requirements."[61] Those prerequisites include preparation and correction of what God reveals in our character. Those aspects can determine whether or not we'll be commissioned. To move from being called to being chosen, we must do much to prepare.

Trials prepare us by building patience, integrity, and love for others. Maybe skills like warfare may be honed. They might teach us to operate in *shama*. Elisha demonstrated how we should respond to our callings. When Elijah threw the mantle over his successor, Elisha chose to move toward fulfillment of his calling. His training took years of servanthood to learn what he'd need to know in order to fulfill his own destiny after his mentor was carried away in the chariot. That season prepared Elisha for his double-portion ministry (2 Ki. 2:9). Paul also teaches about callings. He says God "has saved us and called us with a holy calling, not according to our works, but according to His own purpose and grace which was given to us in Christ Jesus before time began" (2 Tim. 1:9). If, like Elisha, Paul, and others, we accept the charge to fulfill God's holy purpose for us, we must prepare. We'll be ready for God to move us into our commissions.

One major aspect of preparation is time. Saul and David exemplify this principle. Samuel anointed both to be king. Shortly afterwards, Saul was installed in that office but was largely a failure. David, however, endured nearly twenty years of often-difficult preparation. Along the way he was given smaller commissions which also affected his ultimate destiny—shepherd, worshiper, captain, king of Judah. Sometimes those pre-commission commissions may be full-time ministry; often they're simple roles which play a great part in our preparation process. Time allowed God to eliminate from or incorporate into David's character the leadership traits that would serve his kingship well or poorly when he would shepherd a whole nation. His call came around age fifteen, and he ruled all Israel when he was nearly forty (see 2 Sam. 5:4). The Lord has much to do in us before we can begin our commissions. If we don't go through the character-building journey, we won't be prepared. Those preparation years are crucial to whom we will become.

CHAPTER SIX

Worship

THE IMPORTANCE

Worship *must* accompany any *higher* journey. When I dreamed about the piano at our Ohio house, I understood its meaning. I worship at a piano, usually into the glory. True worship proclaims your love for the Lord, not just from your lips but also from your heart. When scribes and Pharisees criticized Jesus, He said, "These people draw near to Me with their mouth, and honor Me with their lips, but their heart is far from Me" (Matt. 15:8). God is seeking those who "will worship the Father in spirit and truth" (Jn. 4:23). He knows our hearts' motives, even in worship (see Mal. 1:8–11). When we honor Him just because we love Him, that's truly speaking to the Master and singing from our hearts. God rejoices over us with singing (see Zeph. 3:17)!

When Jesus said Mary had chosen the good part, He was referring to her focus on worship and adoration of Him (see Lk. 10:38–42). Though Martha's role as a server was/is important in every house or church, this story teaches a crucial message. Serving the Lord in all capacities is vital, but we must prioritize. We give Him worship; then we offer our service. Worship is about devoting time to exalt Him. His glory coming through worship is a treasure, our direct link to God.

WHAT IT IS

Worship is important to a Christian walk and crucial to a *higher* journey. It's demonstrated by many different actions—singing, dancing, shouting, giving, waving our hands, washing His feet, or many other ways. He wants true worshipers, those who sing and speak with "psalms . . . hymns and spiritual songs, singing and making melody in [their] heart[s] to the Lord" (Eph. 5:19). It isn't just about singing or angels or a great worship leader. It's more than going to church on Sundays and hearing good songs by good singers. It's more than passively listening as the worship team leads the congregation. It's more than liking songs selected or appreciating the worship leader's talent. It's not about talent, what type of music, or when we do it. It's not about the pastor or even the worship service itself. It's about participating rather than observing. It's about adoration of Father because we simply and totally love Him. It's about the anointing and knowing we're not trying to please an audience. Instead of singing so others can follow our lead, we should worship so He's delighted. It's about an audience of ONE.

The first biblical use of the word *worship* is when God gave Abraham a difficult assignment: sacrifice his beloved Isaac. The next morning, Abraham readied himself, his men, and his son and went on the three-day journey toward Moriah. When he saw the destination, he said he'd "go yonder and worship" (Gen. 22:5). That tells me that one aspect of worship is sacrifice. That may include giving up a favorite television show or the busyness of our day to spend time with our wonderful Father. Abraham's incident also shows the importance of submission as part of our worship. Again, it's listening with obedience, *shama*. It's acknowledging God as we hear Him and then acting without hesitation because delayed obedience is disobedience. He wants us to have immediate, unquestioning compliance. That's truly worshiping Father.

PRAISE

Worship is crucial, but so is praise because God is "enthroned in the praises of [His people]" (Ps. 22:3). A difference exists between praise and worship. Praise is often more boisterous and excited. Worship is softer, slower, and simpler with the goal of exalting the Lord in a one-on-one encounter. Praise thanks God for what He's done and will do, while worship celebrates Who God is. Praise ushers us into worship. It breaks barriers and brings victories, especially when coupled with a word about how that victory can be achieved. Joshua's triumph at Jericho included praise. After the seventh trip on the seventh day, people shouted while priests blew trumpets; then walls fell (see Josh. 6:15–20). Praise breaks down seemingly impenetrable barriers.

David was a worshiper, but he praised also. As a matter of fact, he knew that a lifestyle of continual praise was a necessity (see Heb. 13:15). After he became king of all Israel, he understood he had to retrieve the Ark of the Covenant, which had been gone from Jerusalem for seventy years. His predecessor Saul hadn't seen the necessity of recovering it. David, however, had learned that God's presence was crucial. He brought it back to Jerusalem with much pomp, circumstance, and intense dancing. Though his behavior was unacceptable to his wife Michal, he said he'd continue to praise even more radically because the Lord had chosen him as king. David's attitude of praise brought him much wealth in his life and kingship, but his wife remained infertile (see 2 Sam. 6:1–23). Not praising and worshiping brings barrenness of spirit.

Jehoshaphat, king of Judah, also demonstrated praise's importance. When word came that a great army was amassing against him, he sought the Lord and called for corporate fasting and prayer. He told the Lord that even if disaster transpired, they'd stand in His presence (see 2 Chron. 20:9). The Lord answered through a prophetic word that "the battle is not yours, but God's" (see 2 Chron. 20:15). The next morning, Jehoshaphat sent singers out before the army, and God set up ambushes against the enemy. Their victory was so great that gathering spoils took three days. After they won the battle, they didn't forget intense praise and worship to the Lord for His great victory (see 2 Chron. 20:1–28). Praise wins unwinnable battles.

Another time, Jehoshaphat went to war with Moab's evil king. Circumstances looked bleak after they'd marched seven days with no water for men or animals. Jehoshaphat asked a question he'd asked before—"Is there no prophet of the Lord here, that we may inquire of the Lord by him?" (1 Ki. 22:7; 2 Ki. 3:11). Jehoshaphat knew their strength, power, and provision came by words from God. They went to the prophet Elisha, who received revelation for victory from the Lord. They obeyed God's direction, and the enemy was defeated (see 2 Ki. 3:9–26). God's guidance provides warfare instructions as a fruit of praise and worship.

Father also fights for us as we praise. Isaiah says that as we face enemies, each blow "the Lord will lay on them, will be to the music of Israel's tambourines and lyres" (Isa. 30:32). In other words, He metes out punishment to correlate with praise. I love the wording of a different translation: "Every passing stroke of the staff of punishment and doom which the Lord lays upon them shall be to the sound of [Israel's] timbrels and lyres, when in battle He attacks [Assyria] with swinging and menacing arms" (Isa. 30:32

AMPC). Imagine how the enemy runs when he sees the Lord's "swinging and menacing arms." Do you need victory? Praise Him with all you have.

EVEN NATURE

God created all things to praise and worship Him. As Jesus made His triumphal entry into Jerusalem, He was met with disciples rejoicing and praising loudly because of His mighty works. They shouted, "Peace in heaven and glory in the highest!" This use of *glory* is *doxa*, "glory (as very apparent) . . . honour, praise, worship."[62] When Pharisees objected to the praise, Jesus told them that if those worshipers would be quiet rather than praise Him, "the stones would immediately cry out" (Lk. 19:38–40). All creation was made by and for God, and even nature's obedience is crucial.

A story about the Ark of the Covenant, God's presence, shows nature's need to worship. After Philistines captured it, the Ark proved to be a curse. They ultimately set it on a cart pulled by milk cows and sent it down the road toward Hebrew territory. The Philistines purposely chose animals which would fail—the cows had never been yoked before, weren't trained to pull, and had babies at home. Despite this, the yoked cows went directly toward Judah and stopped by a rock. Even though their natures could've deterred them from responding this way, their innate need to worship superseded obligations and proclivities. They stopped at that rock because they knew they must worship their Creator. *They* became the sacrifice to their Lord (see 1 Sam. 6:10–14).

Though that necessity is deep inside our nature, too, we often let our human character take precedence over our inborn nature to worship. We're told to offer ourselves as "a living sacrifice [and that is our] reasonable service" (see Rom. 12:1). The word for *service* is *latreia*, which has several meanings including "worship."[63] Worship is our *reasonable* service. Cows and stones and fish and trees and humans and angels and everything else were created to worship. We sacrifice our desires and declare our inner being as we worship in obedience.

I have a friend who begins each morning calling out to *Yahweh*. She comes downstairs; goes into the backyard; lifts both arms; and with hands extended sings in a piercing voice, "*Yahweh!*" When she does that, her hungry chickens pause in reverence to Him, too. They begin to cluck as they join her song to their beloved Creator. She continues a while before she gives her charges their breakfast. When she worships inside, one of them,

Henny Penny, comes to the window by her piano and sings along with my friend. Beginning the morning this way brings anointing into her yard, home, and spirit and carries her through the day.

AN UNBREAKABLE APPOINTMENT

We all need to spend time in worship to glorify and enjoy God's presence. We shouldn't be inhibited by who's looking, judging, or making fun. When people in His own country heard Jesus teach, many "were offended at Him" (Mk. 6:3). What He said and did weren't what people thought should happen, but His will was to do Father's will and way despite others' reactions. Being in God's presence is being in the glory, and that's always been His plan. Worship is the gate to the glory. During this journey, though I knew the importance of worship, I often fell short in regularly devoting time for that precious act. I worshiped erratically, not consistently. Instead of my worship time being an unbreakable commitment, it was frequently an after-thought. Finally, after many broken appointments, I asked Holy Spirit to show me how to remember this important aspect of my journey. He impressed me to include it in morning devotions.

This revelation helped fulfill part of my dream which sent me on my *higher* journey. The first day I began that routine, a sweet presence entered my office. As days of worship continued, I looked forward to the joy of meeting Him and receiving revelations. One morning, I finished my Bible reading and went to my keyboard. I sat down and realized I was smiling in anticipation of my time with Father. I recalled when my girls were about three, and we were dancing at a wedding reception. When their dad said we needed to leave, I told them we had time for one more dance. I spun Jennifer around, and she tilted her head back to look up at me.

"Mommy, when we get home, can we dance some more?" As I remembered Jennifer's words that morning, I felt the same joy and excitement about spending intimate time with my Lord. That morning as I worshiped, an intense, strong presence invaded the room, and I saw two visions:

> *First, I was dancing with Him. He spun me around; and, like Jennifer, I looked up at Him with adoration and joy. In the second vision, He and I were walking together and holding hands, feeling utter peace and contentment as we journeyed.*

That morning, I knew both those revelations happened because I entered His presence through worship, not as a duty but as a joy.

MORNING WORSHIP

After a few days of worshiping alone, Wade joined me. Both of us basked in His gentle presence each morning. A couple weeks later, I felt led to worship on Zoom and invited people who might be interested. We settled on a time that could include those who were in different time zones and ended up with a small group which hungered to be in His presence. We've met each weekday for more than a year now, and each of us who attends regularly has the same comment—our lives have changed. In addition to loving on God, we've had amazing revelations.

One morning, Anita, had come from Arizona to Ohio and stayed all night with us. Though she usually joined online, that morning I let her sleep because she'd just made the long flight. I left my office door ajar; but the bedroom where she slept was two rooms away, so I didn't think she'd be awakened. However, she awoke to our worship, but amazingly she heard more. In the walls of the bedroom, she heard heavenly, masculine voices humming along with worship. Wow! If you want a higher experience that angels attend, worship regularly.

Another time during morning worship, Holy Spirit helped me overcome a problem. A couple nights earlier, I'd been lying in bed, unable to sleep. I saw this vision:

> *With both my hands, I was holding a small wooden box about the size of a jewelry box. On the top was written the word TOXIC.*

I wasn't sure what that referred to. I knew people in toxic relationships, so I prayed for them. The next day when a friend encountered poison oak and had an allergic reaction, I again thought that may have been the toxic meaning. Though it was probably both, the following morning Holy Spirit's message to me became clear while we sat in His presence after worship:

> *Jesus was on the cross. The four of us who worshiped that morning were standing beneath the cross, and blood was dripping onto our heads. We raised our cupped hands to let His blood fill them. I knew that blood was for anything we needed but also for us to pass along for others' needs.*

As I watched this vision unfold, I realized my hands were in the same position as others who were worshiping, but I still held onto the toxic box. I couldn't keep what was noxious in me if I wanted His blood to fill my hands. A jewelry box is meant to hold precious, not lethal items. Though I thought I'd let go of past offenses, I'd been nursing them again. I determined to release that poison forever. When I was reminded of past, hurtful acts, I held up my cupped hands for the Lord to take away the toxic and replace it with His blood. How can we go higher, even in worship, if toxicity in our character doesn't allow us to draw closer as we're covered by His blood?

Other amazing events have occurred during Zoom worship. A lady who joins regularly requested prayer for her pregnant daughter-in-law. She was due in more than a month, and doctors were monitoring her because of difficulties in her first pregnancy. One morning she'd begun contractions, and doctors were trying to stop them. As we sat in God's presence post-worship:

> *I saw a beautifully wrapped package. But a hand put a bow on the side of the package, not the top.*

At first, I didn't say what I thought it meant until another lady said she felt the baby was going to be born early, not when the doctors would've preferred. That resonated with what I thought the Lord was saying to me. The beautiful gift would be born, but not how they'd expected. That's what happened. After a C-section, doctors discovered the placenta had an infection. If they had waited, the baby would've likely died and perhaps the mother as well. God is good!

THE GLORY

Worship is the pathway into God's presence, His glory, and appears in several ways. One morning in His presence, Holy Spirit showed me a light too brilliant to watch. We'd recently experienced a total eclipse with an intensity that couldn't be viewed without shielding our eyes. The Lord reminded me that an eclipse is a fraction of His glory's brightness. God told Moses it was so powerful he couldn't see God's face and live, so He put Moses in the cleft of the rock (see Exod. 33:20–22). His face became so brilliant that he had to wear a veil around people. When Moses went before the Lord in the tabernacle of meeting, he took the veil off; but when he entered God's presence, he'd put it back on. Moses would hear from God then "speak to the children of Israel whatever he had been commanded" (Exod. 34:34). Going into God's presence means all pretense is gone, and He can give direction and revelation.

Moses built the tabernacle to worship God, and its sections demonstrate progression into the glory. The first section was the Outer Court, signifying the beginning of our Christian walk. Implements were set up for worship. The second section was the Holy Place, representing growing deeper in the Lord. It includes being filled with Holy Spirit, but more is available as we step into the Holy of Holies which was separated from the people by a heavy veil. That's where God's presence resided, but now no separation exists because Jesus' death tore down that veil to allow access into God's glory. We can come boldly into His presence.

WHEN WE LEAST FEEL LIKE IT

David said, "Because your steadfast love is better than life, my lips will praise you. So I will bless you as long as I live . . . . My soul will be satisfied . . . and my mouth will praise you with joyful lips" (Ps. 63:3–5 ESV). When we learn that true worship is more than singing, God's presence becomes our passion. Lives change because the latent need to worship becomes dominant. One of the best times to worship is when we least feel like it. Despite what's going on, His "steadfast love" is the answer to all dilemmas. Showing adoration only on Sunday is neglecting a daily connection between us and Father which brings joyful, not sad lips. Finding gladness in trials or whatever the enemy throws at us is a product of worship. Many demonstrate that concept.

Habakkuk said, though everything was falling apart, "Yet I will rejoice in the Lord, I will joy in the God of my salvation" (Hab. 3:17–18). Job worshiped in his darkest times. He'd lost nearly everything, yet he fell to the ground and honored God (see Job 1:20). David worshiped despite trials—Saul's attacks, a child's death, betrayal by his son (see 1 Sam. 18:10; 2 Sam. 12:20; 15:32). That's why God described him as a "man after His own heart" (1 Sam. 13:14). Worship was so important to David that he wrote seventy-three of the 150 psalms and invented worship instruments (see Amos 6:5). When we're sorrowful, worship gives "beauty for ashes, the oil of joy for mourning, [and] the garment of praise for the spirit of heaviness" (Isa. 61:3). No matter the loss or hardship, worship is the answer. Then, our spirit aligns with God's Spirit.

PART TWO | EZEKIEL'S JOURNEY

THE EAST GATE

Ezekiel shows a connection with worship. He's sometimes called "The father of Judaism" because of his later influence on Israel's worship.[64] After Jerusalem had been captured for fourteen years, the LORD's hand came to Ezekiel through the vision culminating in the temple description. A man with a bronze appearance led Ezekiel (see 40:1–3). This description indicates an angel.[65] In several references, as he was shown the temple and its dimensions, the angel brought him to the gate that faced east. He said "the glory of the God of Israel came from the way of the east" (see 43:1–2, for example). That direction and gate represent worship (see Neh. 3:29).

The whole earth can demonstrate His glory as we enter the gate of worship. As Ezekiel fell on his face, he repeated that "the glory of the Lord came into the temple by way of the gate which faces toward the east" (Ezek. 43:4). Ezekiel was lifted by the Spirit and taken into the Inner Court where the LORD's glory filled the temple (see 43:5). Later, Ezekiel says that when we come in through one gate, we should leave through another (see 46:9). When we worship, we're changed.

THE RIVER

Other times, Ezekiel's revelation began with worship. In his river analogy in Chapter 47, he went to the back door of the temple. Water flowed east from under the temple's threshold, south of the altar. A man (angel) led Ezekiel to the temple's north gate and went around the outside to another gate facing east. Water was again running out. The angel with Ezekiel went east with a measuring line (see Ezek. 47:1–3). This description is similar to the gushing into our basement in my first dream. As Holy Spirit's waters flow, different levels of glory attend the depth of our progression and degree of worship.

Ezekiel waded through ankle-deep water, but he went farther into the knee-deep. He and the angel proceeded into waist-deep water. Finally, that water became a deluge, a river he couldn't cross. Its deep waters were to swim in, a gushing where he couldn't put his feet down. When the river reached the sea, waters held healing (see Ezek. 47:3–9). When we go into deeper waters, miracles happen as we give control to Holy Spirit to take us where He desires like He did for the living creatures and their wheels. After we get into the deep water realm, great miracles are inevitable. By the way, with each level the angel "brought [Ezekiel] through" (47:3, for example). As we progress, God's angels accompany us through each stage toward *higher*.

Ezekiel's river, which flowed in increments, describes growth in the Lord. We progress in steps until we're mature enough to give everything to Him. Like Ezekiel's river, various levels allow us to advance from shallow water to a higher spiritual plane. As adoration for Father arises, we go higher and deeper. That message was similar to John's while on the Isle of Patmos. He was given a reed as a measuring rod to gauge the temple, altar, and worshipers (see Rev. 11:1). Moses said worship and compliance to God's directives—His way—draw the glory (see Lev. 9:5-6) and thus relationship with Father. The river teaches much about worship's role in *higher*.

STAIRS

The Lord wants our higher journey to be continuous. After Jerusalem had been captured fourteen years, the hand of the Lord came to Ezekiel in the vision that began the temple tour. As I've said before, they entered the temple through the gate which faced east, but that gate's entrance also included stairs (see 40:6). God had given me my dream and visions of stairs which started my *higher* quest. He communicated this message often. In my journey's first year, I worshiped at home and sat in His presence to soak when I saw my earlier vision:

> *Again, Jesus was standing on the platform's top. Again, He was holding His hands out to me. I hadn't advanced to the first step, but the toe of my shoe rested on it.*

Though my *higher* revelation had been months earlier, I hadn't gone up even one whole step. Holy Spirit's message was either that I had made a little headway or that I was just toying with the idea of *higher*. Either way, I needed to get serious about moving *higher*. I later saw other visions of Jesus on those stairs with some variations. Each time, He stood on the top with His hands welcoming me higher. In a later vision, my whole foot rested on the bottom step. I was going forward tentatively, but I still needed to proceed diligently instead of staying where I was comfortable. I wanted to be totally planted on a higher step.

By year's end, I saw the vision again. My foot was on the second step. As a result of my advancing, I saw another vision:

Jesus wasn't dressed in a carpenter's white attire but a King's magnificence. His long, flaring robe wasn't fabric but a cloud of glory crafted with different sections, patterns, and colors. Designs adorned the panels, but I couldn't tell what those shapes were. In the earlier vision, He held out His hands to me. Now, He was reaching toward me, but I didn't have a platform or steps to climb. Jesus was at the top of the riser, but I was no longer resting my foot on a step. I was lying at His feet in homage to Him.

It was again about worship. This vision reminded me of when John heard the Lord say, "Come up here, and I will show you things which must take place after this" (Rev. 4:1). My getting closer to Him brought Him closer to me. Drawing nearer to Him gave me revelation and changed my perception of Him. I climbed higher as I humbled myself in worship. Lying at His feet changes situations and transforms us. Over the next few months, incidents hindered my climbing higher. However, I still had several *higher* experiences. As I've continued this book, I've gotten a renewed message about going into God's presence through the gate of worship. *Higher* begins there.

CHAPTER SEVEN
Ezekiel, the Commission

EAT THE SCROLL

God's hand gave Ezekiel the scroll. For something as important as Ezekiel's call and glory experiences, God Himself presented the scroll. That type of ancient document was written on animal skins sewn together to create one long piece rolled from the ends. Scrolls were common during that time, but they were usually written on one side only.[66] As the scroll was spread out for Ezekiel, the front and back both had writing with lamentations, mourning, and woe (see 2:9–10). *Lamentations* is a strong word, *qiynah*, which means "a dirge (as accompanied by beating the breasts or on instruments)."[67] This intense reference shows Ezekiel's eventual despair for the plight of the rebellious. That writing may have been on two sides to acknowledge the "abundance of calamities" that would befall Israel,[68] the fullness of God's message about their sin's consequences,[69] the depth of the nation's sins, or the Lord's grief because of that sin. John also saw a scroll with writing on the inside and back (see Rev. 5:1). When a document is covered on both sides, it's established. Nothing can be added to God's Word.[70]

Chapters One and Two were extraordinary examples of Ezekiel's glory experiences. In Chapter Two, God told Ezekiel to open his mouth and eat what He gave him (see 2:8). In Chapter Three, when He handed Ezekiel the scroll, He said to "eat this scroll, and go, speak to the house of Israel" (3:1). Jeremiah had a similar experience when the Lord touched his mouth and said, "Behold, I have put My words in your mouth" (Jer. 1:9). Isaiah had a mouth experience, too, when the Lord called him as a prophet, and an angel touched his mouth with a coal (see Isa. 6:6-7). Though Isaiah's lips were touched, and words were placed in Jeremiah's mouth, God handed His Word to Ezekiel to eat. The difference seems important. God was telling Ezekiel to prepare for his destiny by putting the word inside his essence. Each message the Lord gives to share with others must first be heard and received into our own hearts (see 3:10-11). If we take it all in, eat it, and digest what God has said, we can better impart it to others.[71]

God's handing Ezekiel the scroll was part of his training process for destiny preparation. As we study for and move into our commissioning, we must eat the scroll, His Word. The symbolic act of consuming it could mean we must have the Word in us *before* God gives us our commission. If we don't hunger for and consume His Word, our destinies will be less fruitful or fail altogether. Whether the written Word or a prophetic word, as we internalize His message, absorb it into our spirits, and assimilate it into our thinking, His words and their implications fill our spirits, souls, and bodies. We can understand God on a superficial level; but when we experience relationship and put His word inside us, He becomes a reality. If others see that we know His Word, they'll be more likely to integrate the message from Him into their own lives and hearts.[72] If we have God's revelation in our intellect only, others will know and won't be inclined to internalize the message.

A CRASH COURSE

A few months before Ezekiel received his word from God, Jeremiah gave similar warnings to the captives[73] (see Jer. 29). Jeremiah and Ezekiel were contemporaries and priests who both received calls to be prophets. Along with Daniel, they were prophets in captivity after Israel and Judah had been conquered.[74] These men spoke what the Lord gave, but the prophets' messages differed. Isaiah focused on salvation; Jeremiah preached about judgment, and Daniel taught about the Lord's Kingdom. Ezekiel spoke to the nation as most Old Testament prophets did, but he also called for individual responsibility.[75] Another difference between him and other prophets was that Ezekiel's ministry was immersed in the Lord's glory.[76] He literally saw that glory frequently unfold, in the first three chapters and throughout the rest of his book. Though these experiences make his writings challenging to study, they're a blueprint for those longing for *higher*.

Ezekiel, the Commission

During Ezekiel's first chapters, he'd change from prophet-in-training to prophet. In the Old Testament, prophets-in-training were known as sons of the prophets. Schools were established to teach how to operate as a prophet. Samuel, Elijah, Elisha, and perhaps others were instructors over those would-be prophets (see 1 Sam. 19:20; 2 Ki. 2). Ezekiel, however, didn't have lengthy or formal training but rather a crash course from God. As I mentioned with David and Saul, generally a long preparation time is crucial. However when God grooms us, He's thorough and perfect. That should encourage us as we step into God's purpose. Despite his atypical calling process, Ezekiel's commission was vital and important to him. In later chapters he reflected about how the prophet's responsibility was to be true to God's word.

HARDER THAN FLINT

Ezekiel was to eat the scroll then speak to Israel. He did as God asked and filled his belly with it (see 3:1–3). The belly was considered "the seat of [man's] emotions."[77] When Ezekiel took in the Word, his feelings were included in everything that action would impact. Sometimes as God gives commissions, we're ready in our spirits. We may have our bodies under subjection, but too often we let emotions run rampant. "Will they like what I say?" "Will they accept my prophecy?" "Will I be shunned?" Ezekiel's assignment could create adverse emotions within him. Regardless, God said to speak His word to Israel (see 3:3–4).

God equips His prophets for whatever they'll encounter after accepting a commission. He reminded Ezekiel that he'd speak to the sinful—His rebellious, impudent, and hard-hearted children. However despite the rebellious dynamics, messages from God would be stronger than their stubborn attitudes. If Ezekiel had been called to those of other tongues (foreigners), the Lord said they would've been more receptive (see 3:6). This foreshadows how in the New Testament, salvation was given to the Gentiles because Israel rejected the Lord (see 1 Cor. 14:21). It also mentions other tongues, foretelling of Holy Spirit's coming with tongues in Acts 2.

To be strong in dealing with their rebellious characters, God called Ezekiel to a hard-head anointing. He said He'd made Ezekiel's forehead "like adamant stone" (3:9). *Adamant* is *shamiyr*, "a gem, prob[ably] the diamond."[78] In those days, diamonds scratched flint, a very hard stone. Ezekiel's adamant attitude could pierce hearts as hard as flint.[79] His diamond forehead was stronger than their rebellious, flint attitudes. We can be tough, and that strength is beautiful and precious. However another meaning of *shamiyr* is "brier."[80] God had warned Ezekiel that he'd encounter hurtful briers, but they would prepare him to fulfill his calling. Though we may not see how briers are refining us, we're being shaped into diamonds to cut through difficult messes. If we start our destiny journey with the mindset that we'll encounter briers along the road, we understand that everything that happens to us will shape us into someone God can use for His plan.

Despite knowing that his own people's rejection would cause him pain, Ezekiel readily accepted the call. God prepared him by strengthening him several ways:

1. His face to be strong against their faces (see 3:8)
2. His forehead to be strong against theirs
3. His adamant forehead to become harder than flint (see 3:8–9)
4. His watchman's role to be fulfilled (see 3:17).[81]

God would divinely strengthen Ezekiel to endure even if another person accosted him. The meaning of Ezekiel's name, "strength of God,"[82] prophesied his pathway. People he'd speak to were "literally rebellion itself—rebellion personified,"[83] yet God would enable and strengthen him.

Then, God ended with more encouraging words— "Do not afraid of them, nor be dismayed at their looks" (3:9). When our confidence lies in God, we can rest despite what our eyes see. How wonderful that God again addressed Ezekiel's potentially negative emotional response. Be strong and don't be afraid! When God says not to be afraid, we're going to be okay. After the Lord reinforced the message about going to a rebellious Israel, He indicated why that hard-head anointing was important. People whom Ezekiel would go to were God's anointed nation whose rebellion had led them into captivity. If they'd rebelled against God, Ezekiel could be sure they'd rebel against God's message through him. God had "permit[ed] circumstances . . . which [would] draw out the governing principles of that life."[84] Those principles are to love the Lord with all our heart, mind, soul, and strength (see Lk. 10:27). And to obey.

NOISES

After God gave instructions, another glory manifestation occurred. Holy Spirit again lifted Ezekiel. A "great thunderous [rushing in KJV] voice" said, "Blessed is the glory [*kabod*] of the Lord from His place" (Ezek. 3:12). The use of the word *rushing* makes me again think of Holy Spirit on the Day of Pentecost when a "sound [came] from heaven, as of a rushing mighty wind" (Acts 2:2). That *sound* in the Upper Room was *echos*, "a loud or confused noise."[85] Holy Spirit wasn't still and small but earth-shaking. Ironically, this section of Ezekiel would have been read by Jews at Pentecost.[86] How astounding that probably as they were quoting Ezekiel's passage, Father sent an illustration to those in the Upper Room of how that noise sounded to the prophet. Holy Spirit still sends revelations, signs, and wonders like rushing winds.

Thunderous was *ra'ash*, a "commotion, confused noise, earthquake, fierceness, quaking, rattling, rushing, shaking."[87] Ezekiel was likely startled by the great noise like thunder, but this clamor happened elsewhere in the Bible. Once God wanted to have a personal experience with His people in the wilderness. Three days after Moses told them to consecrate themselves, a thick cloud came, along with thundering, lightning, and a loud trumpet sound. Everything was so piercing that people trembled (see Exod. 19:14–16).

Other glory events appeared as earthquakes accompanied by great noise. At Jesus' resurrection, an angel rolled away the stone and sat on it, which caused an earthquake (see Matt. 28:2). Paul and Silas were jailed for preaching about Jesus. While in prison, they prayed, praised, and sang. Singing to the Lord changes things. At midnight, an earthquake shook the jail so intensely that chains fell off prisoners and cell doors opened (see Acts 16:24–26). Can you imagine the noise of that earthquake, rattling of chains, and ensuing panic? Can you imagine Ezekiel's response when again he had another virtually impossible experience as he heard those sounds?

Angels accompanied Ezekiel to the next location when Holy Spirit placed him by the River Chebar (see 3:15). He heard other great noises: living creatures' wings touching each other; wheels coming beside them; and a "great, thunderous noise" (3:13). When God sends us on a journey, angels attend us. The *touch* of their wings was *nashaq*, meaning "fastening up . . . to kiss . . . to equip with weapons."[88] That's the same word God spoke to Elijah on the mountain when He said His remnant had never bowed to nor kissed

Baal (see 1 Ki. 19:18). Whomever we kiss equips us with weapons, satan or God. As we kiss God, His armaments are beyond imagination.

SWEET BUT BITTER

As the Spirit again lifted him and took him away, Ezekiel "went in bitterness in the heat of [his] spirit" (Ezek. 3:14). Earlier, God's word and revelation were sweet as honey. Now, they became bitter. This *heat* was *chema*, "anger . . . indignation . . . rage, wrath . . . ."[89] As God gives assignments, we experience joy and wonder at the sweetness of what He entrusts to us. Bitterness may creep in as we undergo sorrow associated with the message. Nevertheless, we must answer, fulfill His call, and let Him fortify us. Even in difficult assignments, we "can do all things through Christ who strengthens [us]" (Phil. 4:13) as He enables us to accomplish what He's given. God guided Ezekiel and supported him with His hand, even though he was to speak tough words. He'll guide and bolster us whether people receive, discard, or persecute us because of those words.

Before Ezekiel's bitter response, God had told him to put the sweet word inside his belly. Now, Ezekiel learned that revelations weren't all sweetness when they foretold of great trials. Likely much of Ezekiel's bitterness reflected "righteous anger against [Israel's] sin."[90] While exiled on the Isle of Patmos, John received a sweet revelation from the Lord, but it was also a hard message for many churches. John was to "take and eat [the book]; and it will make your stomach bitter, but it will be as sweet as honey in your mouth" (Rev. 10:9). Sweet but bitter. Like Ezekiel, the sweetness of God's call lingered as John chewed on it, but afterward bitter reality set in (see Rev. 10:8–10). This reaction from two mighty men of God shows that accepting God's commission will come with both the sugary and sour; our job is to convey God's message and fulfill our commissions to the best of our abilities, regardless of its content.

Ezekiel's calling would include much sorrow as he'd watch God's judgment unfold against the rebellious, but God had already prepared Ezekiel to overcome his emotions. The Lord had warned him about Israel's waywardness, dismissal of His words, and unwillingness to comply with His message. Rejection by those Ezekiel loved and lived among would hurt, especially as he observed those people experience God's wrath. Tough messages are difficult, and prophets face these challenges as a messenger of God's grim message. In reality, "it was always the lot of the prophet to bring a message which opposed the ungodly, a voice which the people did not welcome"[91] (for example, Jer. 1:17-19). God warned Ezekiel of that very thing. Though words and reactions may taste bitter, how sweet that God has chosen us to proclaim His words.

ASTONISHED

Again, the Spirit lifted Ezekiel, took him elsewhere on the River Chebar, and set him down with other captives at Tel Abib. He "remained there astonished among them seven days" (3:15). After his incredible encounters with God's glory, he sat in spiritual shock and wide-eyed amazement, contemplating the enormity of God's words and actions (see 3:14-15). *Astonished* is *shamem,* meaning "to stun . . . stupefy . . . make amazed . . . astonish . . . wonder"[92] That sounds like our reactions to God's powerful signs and wonders.

We should always acknowledge Father for amazing experiences, but reacting with astonishment to signs and wonders is appropriate. Though his prayer group had been intensely interceding for Peter while he was in prison, they were at first skeptical and then astounded and joyful after his supernatural escape (see Acts 12:16). When Eutychus was resurrected, that assembly was "not a little comforted" (Acts 20:12). After Jesus raised Jairus' daughter, onlookers were "overcome with great amazement" (Mk. 5:42). Ezekiel's response at the River Chebar may have been because of all he'd seen, or he may have been stunned by yet another translation. As we experience glory events, reacting with excitement shows wonder and awe. We're "not a little comforted" by experiencing God's astonishing events.

A WATCHMAN

After seven days he'd probably not yet processed what had happened. God outlined his job for the Kingdom—he was to be a watchman for Israel (see 3:17). The number seven represents several things to Hebrews. It's a time of deep mourning for the dead, a period of uncleanness after touching the dead, or a time of consecration as a priest.[93] Though Ezekiel's preparation wasn't as long as most, seven represented his training time with God as his Teacher. What an awe-inspiring start of a destiny! Before God could send him, though, Ezekiel had to agree to answer the call. The commission would require much from him and will for us, too, if we choose to accept or not.

In the first two chapters, God told Ezekiel what his job would entail. Now, He'd assigned that commission. When God gave Ezekiel His *word*, *dabar*, it meant "a matter (as spoken of)...glory...power...sign."[94] These describe what Ezekiel would encounter. God's glory with signs, wonders, and power accompanies His words. During our journey as we await our commissions, we should occupy and work for the Kingdom in different capacities. Like Ezekiel, our ultimate commission will probably differ from our current assignment, but God will use what we've learned at each phase of ministry for our new mission. Ezekiel was a priest who was now commissioned as a prophet to God's rebellious people. He would now sympathize with and warn Israel.[95]

A watchman (prophet) was to sound the alarm and call others to get right with God.[96] Prophets are important in God's plan: "A prophet without a vision from God would be false; a vision without a prophet to herald the Lord's message to man would be useless."[97] God needs prophets to step up and give His pronouncements. Those with a prophet's call on their lives should be willing to speak to others collectively or individually as God leads.

Watchman is *tsaphah*, "to lean forward, i.e., to peer into the distance ...to observe, await: —behold...look up...wait for, (keep) watch."[98] That definition gives a perfect picture of a watchman as he waits with outstretched neck to scan the horizon. *Tsaphah* includes diligence to receive God's word and pass it on. Stationed on the city's walls, an observant watchman could see from an elevated position and give warnings as danger approached.[99] He was to tell of "impending disaster [but also to make a] call to repentance and faith."[100] His message might be bad or good, but he relayed crucial information—messengers or invading armies. Attacks may come from an outside source or from within our own walls—home, job, friend, family, church, etcetera. As watchmen, we should see from His perspective to sound the alarm and alert others. We watchmen must be vigilant and attentive to listen to God's warnings and then pass them along to others.

INTEGRITY

Anyone who desires a higher walk should be aware of integrity's importance. David said, "Who may ascend into the hill of the Lord? Or who may stand in His holy place? He who has clean hands and a pure heart, who has not lifted up his soul to an idol, nor sworn deceitfully" (Ps. 24:3-4). If we want to ascend higher, we must make sure our hands, heart, soul, and mouth are clean. Whatever we do for the Lord reflects on Him, so we should always be cognizant of our character and actions. When God gave Habakkuk his assignment, he said, "I will stand my watch and set myself on the rampart, and watch to see what He will say to me, and what I will answer when I am corrected" (Hab. 2:1). Integrity as a watcher to use our gifts and share God's exact word with others is crucial. Sometimes, though, He doesn't speak about others but shows flaws in ourselves. We should be diligent, listen to, and internalize what He says about us personally and deal with whatever He highlights in us.

Miriam was charged with an important duty as a watcher—to make sure her baby brother Moses wasn't harmed as he floated down the Nile. She fulfilled that calling with integrity. She stayed at her post during the potentially hazardous journey and trailed the baby while he escaped from those who wanted him dead. She continued to watch as he floated farther down the danger-ridden river and ultimately was lifted from it. However, Miriam didn't desert her charge because the princess rescued him. She interceded on his behalf and suggested a Hebrew woman—his actual mother—who not only could nurse the baby but would be paid for it (see Exod. 2:4-7). Her watcher duties were important to what would later unfold for the nation of Israel. Though she was a prophetess and a worship leader, her duty was also to help the prophet as a watcher (see Exod. 15:20). That calling followed her into adult life as she accompanied Moses and his charges toward the Promised Land. As watchers, our job is important on many levels and in many seasons.

TO FULFILL HIS CALL

As Chapter 3 ended, the Lord told Ezekiel, "He who hears, let him hear" (see Ezek. 3:27). As a prophet to the exiles, Ezekiel was to call out personal responsibility and acceptance of God's message.[101] He was to warn of penalties for those who heard but ignored. Jesus also taught that people need to choose to accept or reject His message (see Matt. 11:15). Each person is responsible for his or her obedience, despite many good excuses. Each of us needs to accept Jesus Christ as our personal Savior and give Him total allegiance.

Watchers are not only accountable for their own fates and obedience but also for warning those entrusted to them. God considers watchmen who don't alert people as "manslayer[s]."[102] Isaiah describes irresponsible leaders who are neglectful of their duties as blind, greedy, and ignorant watchers—mute and lazy dogs. They love to sleep, lack understanding, and are self-centered (see Isa. 56:10-12). Jesus called an irresponsible shepherd a "hireling" (Jn. 10:13), one who doesn't really care about his flock's well-being.

One of Ezekiel's words also dealt with those who didn't perform God-given jobs faithfully. He said some shepherds feed and clothe themselves, not the flock. They don't perform their duties such as strengthening, healing, helping the broken, or seeking those who've wandered away. They've ruled cruelly and forcefully (see 34:2-4). He points out that false prophets say words are from God, but they're speaking from their own hearts without seeing anything (see 13:1-3). Others' well-being and destinies are a watchman's responsibility. Again, it's about integrity. Do you know some commissioned as watchers who fail to fulfill their jobs with diligence and integrity?

Charles Spurgeon said, "A time will come when instead of shepherds feeding the sheep, the church will have clowns entertaining the goats."[103] That describes many churches today. Isaiah's, Ezekiel's, Spurgeon's, and Jesus' descriptions sadden me. Whatever God gives, we should accomplish it with seriousness and commitment (see Ecc. 9:10). No small jobs exist for the Kingdom, and undertaking anything for the Lord is an honor not to be taken lightly. Speaking God's judgment, whether harsh or not, is crucial. We shouldn't hold back because of others' potential disapproval, blatant criticism, or rejection. Though Ezekiel's duty was to warn, he wouldn't be responsible for how the message was received (see 3:11). Knowing that results are Holy Spirit's responsibility takes much pressure off us.

ALONE WITH GOD

The hand of the Lord again came on Ezekiel and sent him to the plain, a desert area where Ezekiel and God could be alone and talk. We want to be in His glory but fail to find time to get isolated with Father. All of us need a solitary place and time to converse with the Lord because "He who dwells in the secret place of the Most High shall abide under the shadow of the Almighty" (Ps. 91:1). Even Jesus needed alone time with His Father (see Lk.

6:12). Our lives get so full of "stuff" that communing with Him privately in our secret place is regularly neglected. When we're alone with Father, we gain intimacy as we hear what He has to say.

Ezekiel obeyed: He arose, went, and again saw God's glory. After this, Ezekiel fell on his face (see 3:22–23). The "glory of the Lord stood there, like the glory . . . by the River Chebar" (3:23). That glory was *kabod*, but *stood* is also interesting. It's *amad*, meaning several things, including "abide . . . appoint . . . confirm . . . establish . . . ordain . . . tarry."[104] Ezekiel experienced God's glory by the Chebar before, but the meanings of *amad* show this event's importance. His glory can abide, endure, and tarry with us. Through the glory, God will establish us so that our callings become our commissions. He appoints, confirms, and ordains us like Ezekiel.

Being isolated with God allowed Ezekiel to receive words as he gave himself totally to the Lord. This seclusion reminds us not to leave His presence until God reveals His word to us. Too many fail because they don't wait to hear complete instructions. The action of being separated from others was how Ezekiel's ministry would function. The Lord warned him that he'd be bound and couldn't go among others. Both literally and figuratively, he was to be tied with ropes (see 3:25). This could prevent his assignment from derailing if he proceeded before God gave direction.

TO YOUR HOUSE AND OTHERS

The Spirit entered and set Ezekiel on his feet for a second time (see 2:2; 3:24). God directed him to shut himself in his house. Perhaps that meant Ezekiel should minister to his own house before spreading God's word outside. Our families are part of those for whom we should intercede or give God's messages. If we're called to minister only to our families, what a precious job! But the Lord has so much more for us to accomplish as we help others, many times in a small group setting. The First Century church had home meetings; and many today do, too.

Ministry in intimate venues is extremely valuable and productive. Home gatherings or small groups create familiarity and relationships sometimes lost in larger settings. After Wade and I started a Bible study at our house, attendance grew from fifteen the first night to more than fifty a year later. During that time, Holy Spirit revealed Himself regularly and intensely. Though we eventually moved to larger venues for those meetings, for many years we still offered weekly classes for prayer and teaching from our home, and that started our streaming ministry. During that time, we often saw God's presence and resulting signs and wonders manifest.

MEMORIAL PILLARS

The River Chebar was the location for many of Ezekiel's glory experiences and had become his memorial pillar to recall God's amazing wonders. Memorial pillars aren't a single occurrence but are forged during occasions when God has shown Himself mighty. As we reflect on these times, we're strengthened and encouraged to face hard stretches. We can become disheartened when the road on which Father has sent us is fraught with delays, disagreements, and disappointments. However, memorial pillars are important. Remembering those incidents brings renewed reassurance, trust, and faith. I've mentioned my family's memorial pillars such as our sledding incident. That word which came quietly but firmly to Mom demonstrated a memorial pillar about how Holy Spirit led the Hunter clan through yet another crisis.

Another event impacted my mom's extended family and became a far-reaching memorial pillar. Her sister was suffering from rheumatic heart and had been given a short time to live. In anticipation of impending death, her family had given her an early graduation and Christmas. Then my grandfather walked down a city street and heard animated music emanating from a building. He discovered the source—a theater converted to a church. A healing evangelist was ministering that night, so Grandpa went in to listen to his message of God's love and power—the Healer of whatever we need. Grandpa witnessed many miracles that night. As a result, he gave his heart to God and decided to prove what the preacher had said and God had demonstrated. He planned to take his dying daughter to a healing service. Though my mom adamantly opposed that ride which could kill her sister, she ultimately relented and traveled along.

The service was no longer inside a building but under a tent on the outskirts of town. Comfortable chairs didn't adorn a large cathedral, but planks rested upon stumps. Seeing the less-than-pristine conditions, my defiant mother grew more skeptical; but the Lord didn't need a fancy, cozy environment to heal my aunt. Like those Grandpa had seen at the store-front church, she was healed that night. As a result, my mother and grandfather became forever in love with Jesus, who cared so much that He healed their loved one. Though their family had never been believers, eventually they were all saved. By the way, my aunt lived long enough to see great-grandchildren. That memorial pillar still impacts my family—siblings, children, cousins, and so many more.

BE SILENT

God told Ezekiel to stay secluded. Often we're too interested in associating with others—on social media, the phone, even in church. God wants us to have solitary times to communicate with Him, and He with us. Because Ezekiel wasn't to speak unless God put a word in his mouth, God would make his tongue cling to the roof of his mouth to keep him silent until the Lord gave a word (see 3:26–27). His ministry began with silence rather than speaking. I love this message: Be silent until I speak to and through you. That's good instruction not only to prophets but to all Christians. We may talk way too much, and in a "multitude of words sin is not lacking" (Prov. 10:19). Sometimes that sin includes negativity, unforgiveness, judgment, and gossip. We may speak fear instead of faith or give opinions that impede how God wants to move. For so many reasons, when "the Lord is in His holy temple[,] the earth [should] keep silence before Him" (Hab. 2:20). Our neglecting to "keep silence" until He speaks impacts our *higher* quest.

We witnessed that concept of being still in the nineties during the River Movement. When we visited a Kentucky church, God's glory came regularly and mightily. More than once, a speaker approached the podium to preach his sermon. He'd attempt to speak, but nothing came out. He'd try again, but no sound left his mouth. Sometimes, he'd become frozen and couldn't move his body or close his mouth. God's power erupted visibly with miraculous signs and wonders. Even a stellar sermon in that atmosphere would've impeded the Spirit. God used Ezekiel's silent tongue to illustrate that point—don't speak unless God says. Then, watch God work.

OUR COMMISSIONS

Everyone has a call: the Great Commission—to seek the lost for the Kingdom (see Mk. 16:15). However, a select few receive personal commissions, chosen just for them. Our callings become commissions after we single-mindedly pursue fulfillment of them and let Jesus refine us so we're ready to step into our commission. As I said earlier, that usually happens through time and trials. Often implementation of our commissions comes after desert training like with Jesus, Elijah, and Moses (see Lk. 4:1–14; 1 Ki. 17:2–8; Exod. 3:1–10). Before Jesus began His ministry, He not only had a desert experience, but He also spent time in warfare against satan. After He withstood temptation, angels ministered to Him before His ministry began (see Matt. 4:11). Again, alone time with God creates strength to overcome the enemy who'll rise against us.

When Jesus met Saul on the Road to Damascus, others with him heard a voice but saw no one. Later, he said some witnessed the light but didn't hear the voice (see Acts 9:7; 22:9). This says much. First, no one perceives our callings exactly as we do. Second, when Holy Spirit reveals our calling/commission through a glory event, others will know Father has truly sent us. After Paul and his companions had fallen to the ground in response to the bright light, Jesus' voice spoke for him to rise. He said, "I have appeared to you . . . to make you a minister and a witness both of the things which you have seen and of the things which I will yet reveal to you" (Acts 26:16). Jesus went on to give further details of Saul's ministry (see Acts 26:13–18). Saul/Paul's commissioning and reaction were similar to Ezekiel's. When Ezekiel was in the intense glory by the River Chebar, he fell on his face. After the Spirit set him on his feet, He gave instructions for fulfilling his commission (see 3:23–27).

As part of our DNA, we're given motivational gifts sometimes called Gifts of the Father. Being part of our essence, they play a major role in what we'll become (see Rom. 12:6–8). For our calling, equipping, and commissioning, God considers those motivational gifts, experiences, strengths, personalities, and weaknesses. Like with Ezekiel, during the season between calling and commission, He will:

1. Confirm His vision and His will, often through supernatural occurrences (see 1:1)

2. Position us where we can accomplish His assignment (see 1:1)

3. Encourage and mature us (see 2:6)

4. Reveal His glory (see 1:28).

Then when we go into our commissions, He enables and strengthens us, through giving direction and making His will clear (see 3:8, 5, 24). Holy Spirit empowered Ezekiel to understand and fulfill his commission. It wasn't like any other prophet's assignment. God had chosen it just for him.

For his commission, Ezekiel was given four instructions:

1) Go to the rebellious, impudent nation whether they receive the word or not (see 2:3–3:3)

2 and 3) Hear and receive the Lord's words, and speak them to others (see 3:10–16)

4) Be a watchman to the nation and speak to change their direction (see 3:17–27).[105]

Again, Ezekiel was warned in advance that the rebellious wouldn't listen because they didn't heed God Himself (see 3:7). Ezekiel had to factor their ignoring his message from God into his decision about accepting the commission. The road to destiny can be bumpy and challenging, and we may think the effort isn't worth it. Whatever God has planned is more wonderful than anything we could envision for ourselves.

CHAPTER EIGHT
Count the Cost

Glory occurrences that John, Ezekiel, and others experienced were new and beyond what they could imagine. I'm sure people responded with cynicism and criticism about details they shared. Today many refuse to believe glory events can happen because that particular incident isn't part of their life experiences. When a manifestation occurs and someone says it can't be legitimate because the Bible doesn't mention that particular one, here's my response. John addressed skeptics at the end of his gospel when he said, "there are also many other things that Jesus did, which if they were written one by one . . . even the world itself could not contain the books" (Jn. 21:25). In other words, a lot of possibilities are valid but were left unsaid simply because the Bible didn't have enough room to mention them all.

His glory and power are unimaginable, so why do we limit Him by what our eyes see, our minds comprehend, or our lives experience? I love when Luke quotes Habakkuk: "Behold, you despisers, marvel and perish! For I work a work in your days, a work which you will by no means believe, though one were to declare it to you" (Acts 13:41, from Hab. 1:5). Sounds like today! We should rejoice when we hear about, experience, or witness God's glory. He's working a work that's so special, it's beyond the realm of the ordinary or believable.

SAUL/PAUL

Because others don't understand our *higher* walk, a cost often ensues. After the Damascus Road glory experience, the Lord sent Ananias to Saul. God instructed him to tell Saul how much he'd ultimately suffer if he chose to work for Jesus (see Acts 9:11–16). Saul still followed. From the beginning he determined that whatever the cost, he intended to "press toward the goal for the prize of the upward call of God in Christ Jesus" (Phil. 3:14). That's higher. Even though it was a sacrifice, the wondrous King that Saul encountered on the road completely changed his life forever.

His prize was the fulfillment of that call, but it came at a price. He listed hardships he'd endured because of ministry:

> In labors more abundant, in stripes above measure, in prisons more frequently, in deaths often. From the Jews five times I received forty stripes minus one. Three times I was beaten with rods; once I was stoned; three times I was shipwrecked; a night and a day I have been in the deep; in journeys often, in perils of waters . . . robbers . . . my own countrymen . . . Gentiles [. . . . Also] in perils in the city . . . wilderness . . . sea . . . among false brethren; in weariness and toil, in sleeplessness often, in hunger and thirst, in fastings often, in cold and nakedness—besides the other things. (2 Cor. 11:23–27)

Could we have withstood those adversities and considered them joyfully? Paul saw his call as precious not inconvenient nor too much to ask as he maneuvered through God-given assignments. He was willing to pay the high cost to claim the prize chosen just for him.

JESUS

Jesus also taught about costs. He wondered if His followers would begin to build a tower without considering the cost (see Lk. 14:28). He also addressed the cost with two disciples who wanted to follow Him. Jesus said to the first that to do His ministry, He Himself often suffered hardships. Though foxes and birds had places to live, He had nowhere to call home (see Matt. 8:20). Jesus was warning that answering the call would be an atypical life for those who are chosen. The second disciple wanted to attend to his father's burial; but the Lord said that to follow Him, he must choose Jesus above even family (see Matt. 8:20–22). He expects us to complete what we start and commented that anyone who "put his hand to the plow" but looked back wasn't "fit for the kingdom of God" (Lk. 9:62). That frequently arduous destiny road is a painstaking journey culminating in growth and much reward in His Kingdom. Destiny comes as we continue regardless of the price. Jesus' journey cost Him much, even before His sacrifice on the cross.

During one of His most incredible miracles, Martha approached Jesus about her brother. She wanted Him to realize that if He'd returned when they'd summoned Him, Lazarus' death would have been prevented. Jesus had another plan. At Lazarus' tomb He told Martha, "If you would believe, you would see the glory of God" (Jn. 11:40). They took away the stone, and Lazarus' resurrection became the ultimate glory event (see Jn. 11:20, 38–44). God's glory follows those who believe even in impossibilities like resurrections. Though He endured criticism for returning "late," if Jesus had come back when Martha and others thought He should've, this great event wouldn't have happened.

EZEKIEL

Ezekiel's answering his commission also came at a cost. Words spoken against him would cut and sting. He'd probably be taunted for weird glory experiences he shared. He'd endure disapproving, unkind looks. He'd contend with scorpions, briers, and thorns and dwell among scorpions with deadly poison in their sting (see 2:6–8). A *scorpion* may have been literal or "fig. [uratively] a scourge or knotted whip."[106] He'd be stung by words or perhaps literally beaten with knots braided just for him. As I've said before, those warnings could have made Ezekiel's emotions rise, but his adamant forehead protected him from deserting his watchman's position when those to whom he prophesied refused to act on God-given words (see 2:7). Rejection may create a pitfall for some who operate in the prophetic. Though others' responses can derail us, that hard-head anointing makes us overcomers.

Ezekiel wrote many centuries ago, yet some still attack him. People criticize, judge, and say his writings about the supernatural show he had mental disorders.[107] Rather than denigrating him, we should be inspired by Ezekiel. Having others disparage and condemn didn't deter him from his goal. It shouldn't for us either because it's part of the cost we pay to continue heading higher toward the prize. As we persevere in doing what God gives despite others' perceptions and opinions, our adamant forehead should guide us, not our weak emotional responses.

Ezekiel experienced more costs. He was on the opposite side from people he knew and loved. He endured their impudence and hard-heartedness.

He operated outside his comfort zone. He saw the rebellious perish. He was alienated from others (see 3:4–7, 15, 19–20, 24). He experienced God's warning firsthand: "They hear your words, but they do not do them" (Ezek. 33:32). Because of consequences from his choice to pursue the commission, his human side could have veered from God's message and spoken words from his own heart to be a people-pleaser instead of a speaker of hard truths.

God helped Ezekiel by making him silent to speak only words from the Lord (see 3:26). He was to continue giving God's tough messages—people should turn from both "wickedness . . . [and their] wicked ways" (3:19). That distinction says much. Wickedness describes what's inside while wicked ways result from that wickedness.[108] Ezekiel had to tell his fellow Hebrews that they needed to change both. God again warned Ezekiel that if he didn't fulfill the commission to speak His words to the wicked, their blood would be required at his hand.[109]

Ezekiel willingly accepted these costs, but another price was harder. During his ninth year in exile, Ezekiel's wife died,[110] and he was to "sigh in silence" (24:16) but not mourn her passing (see 24:15–24). Losing one's spouse would be doubly hard without closure for emotional turmoil. People questioned that unusual behavior (see 24:19), but God asked this of Ezekiel to demonstrate a prophetic message. Not being allowed to grieve foretold of the Jerusalem temple's destruction, but people wouldn't be permitted to grieve because of their disobedience.

Though his wife's death was a hard to endure, Ezekiel paid the ultimate cost later in his journey. Though the Bible doesn't record his death, tradition says Ezekiel was murdered by one of his fellow exiles against whom he'd spoken judgment about idol worship. They also blamed him for cursing their children and flocks.[111] Though much sweetness comes from being God's chosen, destiny has a cost.

OUR COST

In the First Century church, God's signs and wonders were demonstrated mightily. People heard about, witnessed, marveled, and esteemed the disciples, but still didn't follow them (see Acts 5:12–13). Many believers today are satisfied knowing that going higher *can* happen but not wanting to press in so it *will* happen. They choose not to pay the cost. Seeking a glory walk isn't a popular road, and ups and downs occur while traveling in territory where little traffic has ventured. Experiencing the glory has come at a cost for us and will for you, too.

Many years ago while reading a book about the glory, I was surprised that people had experienced glory manifestations for a long time. Many gatherings saw jewels, fire, manna, angel feathers, anointing oil, and other unbelievable signs and wonders. Though we know glory events are all about Him and not just the signs and wonders, we were excited when they happened in our classes and services. While we pastored, our little church nestled in an Indiana cornfield saw more than its share of healings and glory occurrences. Hot spots of His presence were located around the podium. Some couldn't walk through that area without being slain in the Spirit. One night, a man had been slain. God led me to have someone blow on his eyes. The man on the floor had been declared legally blind; but when he opened his eyes, he said, "I can see the rafters!"

After we began home meetings, people regularly saw gold dust cover their hands and faces. Also, orbs appeared at our meetings. Another amazing happening occurred. One night a woman at our home Bible study received a gold, cross-shaped filling in her molar (Appendix #5). That wonder then happened to Wade. He discovered brackets which held his back teeth on one side and a new, gold tooth on the other side (see Appendix #6).

As astounded and excited as we were when these and other manifestations occurred, not everyone accepted those wonders as treasures. Many felt they couldn't attend our meetings because we were too "out there." When one pastor heard about Wade's miraculous gold tooth, he pulled back his cheek to show his dental work. He sarcastically said, "I've got a gold tooth, too." A lady watching our streaming program one night refused to join us on Facebook anymore because someone who was attending in person shared that she had gold dust on her hands. Although many wonders and revelations arrived as we worshiped, several people criticized my worship and said I should, "Stay in my lane." Another time when I shared with a friend about an angelic experience, she told me not to tell others because it was too weird.

Wade and I didn't intentionally seek to have signs and wonders trail us. We just trusted in Holy Spirit's omnipotent, unlimited power. Then we made ourselves available. Whenever someone sets aside time to teach about Holy Spirit, He shows up. Those who pursue *higher* don't have to follow signs and wonders. They chase down those who believe (see Mk. 16:17). Despite critics, Wade and I haven't been deterred but have pushed toward *higher*. No matter what, those who experience the supernatural can be in awe and rejoice, even when ridiculed or scorned. Our goal is to go deeper and higher into His presence where the glory dwells. We should take our eyes off what's in the natural and "set [our] mind[s] on things above, not on things on the earth" (Col. 3:2). Because of His radical ways, people in the synagogue in Jesus' hometown were going to throw Him off a cliff. In a glory manifestation, He passed unharmed through their midst (see Lk. 4:28-30). Jesus experienced many glory events and resulting costs during His time on earth. Why shouldn't we?

PART THREE

GLORY PURPOSES

CHAPTER NINE

Reasons for the Glory: Redemptive Names

Ezekiel wasn't the only biblical saint who witnessed the Lord's glory. As I've said before, Saul (Paul) was commissioned after Jesus approached with a bright light, and he later fell into a trance (see Acts 22:7–10, 17–18). Moses was described as communicating with God "face to face, as a man speaks to his friend" (Exod. 33:11). He encountered the glory on a mountain top where God's finger etched His law into a stone (see Exod. 31:18). Isaiah saw the Lord sitting on a high throne lifted up, and His robe's train filled the temple (see Isa. 6:1). No matter what transpires, He's still on His throne with even the direst situation under control.

The Old Testament refers to three fundamental names of God—*Jehovah*, *Adonai*, and *Elohim*. *Yehovah* means Lord and is defined as the "Jewish national name of God."[112] Lord is *Adonai* which stresses His dominance as Master and Head.[113] *Adonai Yahweh* together is read as *Elohiym*, God as the Omnipotent Creator.[114] He's "the supreme God; . . . great . . . x mighty."[115] The two names together—Lord (*Adonai*) and God (*Yahweh*)—are used 217 times in Ezekiel (see Ezek. 2:4, for example). They occur together in the rest of the Old Testament only 103 times.[116] Ezekiel's often using the supreme God's name isn't surprising because he had intimacy with *Elohim* that few others had.

Though these are names of the ONLY God, He's also referred to by various aspects of His Person. As His children's needs arose, His redemptive names describe how He revealed Himself for specific reasons because "God never grants visions of His glory to man without a purpose."[117] God's presence comes for a variety of reasons, and a connection exists between His redemptive names and glory experiences that signal His presence. Through covenants with His people, *Jehovah* revealed more dimensions of His character, and redemptive names represent more than the need He addressed. They describe His character. For example we know God loves us, but He actually *IS* love; He *IS* Healer (*Rapha*); He *IS* Provider (*Jireh*), etcetera. He personifies His names.

JEHOVAH-JIREH

Abraham and Moses

Jehovah-Jireh is the name for God as Provider. He consummately supplies our needs because He sees what we require before we do. *Jehovah* showed this aspect of Provider when He told Abraham to do the unimaginable—sacrifice his son. He didn't react as we would—bemoan and argue with God. Instead, "Abraham rose early in the morning and saddled his donkey" (Gen. 22:3). With two of his men and Isaac, he split wood and journeyed three-days toward Mount Moriah. When they arrived, a confused Isaac asked about the sacrificial lamb (see Gen. 22:3–7). Abraham's response was "God will provide" (Gen. 22:8). The Hebrew word *Jireh* comes from *ra'ah*, a word some Bible versions translate as *provide*. However, *ra'ah* has many meanings including "consider . . . have experience . . . regard, (have) respect."[118] Abraham had experience with and respect for God, but God also respected Abraham.

As he readied his sacrifice, the Angel of the Lord called to Abraham to stop (see Gen. 22:11–12). Abraham's Angel was *malak*, "to despatch as a deputy; a messenger . . . ."[119] *Jehovah Jireh* dispatched His top Angel to provide the much-needed sacrifice. Abraham's sacrifice demonstrates the importance of obedience in receiving God's provision. After following the Angel's direction, Abraham spotted a ram in the thicket. He called this place, "The-Lord-Will-Provide" (Gen. 22:14). Another translation says, "Abraham called the name of that place *Jehovahjireh*" (Gen. 22:14 KJV). *Yehovah Yireh* means "*Jehovah* will see (to it)."[120] Again, *Jehovah Jireh* sees our needs before we ask. What a message! Your family desperately requires a home, an affordable vehicle, or money for bills. *Jehovah-Jireh* will see to it. How He provides may be in many ways—a check in the mail, a call from a friend, a lamb stuck in the bushes. He's our Source no matter the need or means He uses. Jesus said not to worry about what we lack because Father knows (see Matt. 6:31–32). He'll see to it.

Moses also discovered God's character of provision. The Israelites had been in the wilderness for around two years.[121] At Kadesh, they encountered a problem which could've meant many deaths—no water. Of course, with the attitude they'd already perfected, the Israelites grumbled, complained, and blamed Moses. That pattern would follow them for the rest of their decades of wandering. However, instead of being discouraged by hardship or others' negativity, Moses and Aaron went to the Lord. *Jehovah's* glory appeared again for a purpose—to provide. God told Moses to speak to the rock, and water would emerge. Though Moses trusted God, he struck the rock instead and paid a great price. God provided; but because Moses' actions didn't hallow the Lord for others to see, Moses couldn't complete the journey into the Promised Land (see Num. 20:1–12). God loves to do good things for His kids and sends His glory for that purpose. In return, He expects obedience and reverence.

PROVISION

Jehovah-Jireh will see to it and may provide in simple ways. My Aunt Sherrie needed to rely on this knowledge when she and her son relocated across the country to Los Angeles, away from most of her family. Because of that move, family wasn't around to help when she was diagnosed with an autoimmune disease which resulted in her losing her job. Though her disease was miraculously healed by *Jehovah-Rapha* in a month, growing strong enough to work again took nearly a year. Just a short distance from her apartment were lavish homes, restaurants where diners' meals cost more than her rent, and sunbathers tanning on beaches without a thought of those like my aunt who couldn't afford to feed herself and her young son Brian. Although she had nothing in her bank account, Sherrie knew God would provide.

One day their bare cupboards and refrigerator taunted them and tested her faith. Knowing their situation, Brian burst in after school about 3:00. "What're we gonna eat?" he asked, tears filling his hazel eyes and his tummy growling loud and long.

She spoke what Abraham had said all those years before: "God will provide." She smiled hoping to receive a grin in return. When he despondently sat as if his world were falling apart, she asked, "If you had your choice of anything to eat, what would it be?"

Without hesitation, he answered, "Chicken and rice!" They paused a moment and thought of that impossible dream. Attempting to keep his mind off his belly, Sherrie sent him outside to play, but he repeatedly returned. With each outdoor stint, his hunger drew him back in, but she again directed him outside. With false bravado, she assured him she'd call when dinner was ready.

She'd always believed we should do what we can and let Father do the rest. She got out her frying pan and waited. And waited. She could've given up as minutes slowly crawled by; but she'd encountered *Jehovah-Jireh* before, so she acted in faith. Finally, when Brian came in again and proclaimed even louder that he was hungry, she told him to set the table. After he finished, they sat down and waited. And waited some more.

Around 7:00, a knock broke the silence. They looked at each other and hurried to answer the door. A neighbor stood there, sheepishly holding a covered pot.

"We had extra for dinner. Would you like some?" My aunt smiled, extended her hands, and thanked the woman profusely. Brian stared intently at their neighbor and then at the covered pot. His mouth was open in disbelief as he processed what had just happened. After she'd passed the container to Sherrie, the neighbor turned to walk away. She paused and looked back at Sherrie. "Oh, it's chicken and rice."

As they closed the door, both Sherrie and Brian began to cry. They sat down, gave thanks for this miracle, and ravenously dug in. They ate it all—even the last morsel of rice. Between bites they talked about God's goodness, especially when their situation looked the darkest.

Then Sherrie asked, "You know what would be good right now? Chocolate cake! And a big glass of ice-cold milk!" Brian smiled and closed his eyes, tasting this remarkable-yet-unrealistic dream. Suddenly, another knock broke the silence.

The same neighbor was back, balancing a cake dish in one hand and a carton of milk in the other. "We also had leftover dessert. Chocolate cake. And I brought milk. Are you interested?"

My aunt and her son broke into sobs in front of their benefactor. Just as the Lord had provided Abraham a ram in the thicket, *Jehovah-Jireh* provided chicken, rice, chocolate cake, and milk to a starving, desperate family. He gave them not only their needs but also their desires. When God's glory comes to provide, it may not be in a whirlwind or a chariot of fire, but sometimes as a neighbor bearing leftovers.

JEHOVAH-RAPHA—THE LORD OUR HEALER

Jehovah revealed another aspect of His character to His people—*Jehovah-Rapha*, "the Lord who heals." Like *Jehovah-Rapha* healed my aunt, He heals now as He did in Bible times. Those healings aren't just physical. Shortly after the Hebrews had gone through the Red Sea, they went to the Wilderness of Shur where they traveled three days without water. At Marah, when they saw water, sorrow turned into rejoicing until they discovered it was poisoned. When people again bemoaned their fate, Moses obeyed God's revelation and threw a tree into the water thereby healing it. God made a promise. If they diligently obeyed Him, none of the Egyptians' diseases would come on them for "I am the Lord who heals you" (Exod. 15:26). *Heals* is *rapha*, to "mend . . . cure . . . heal . . . repair . . . make whole."[122]

I love each meaning, especially to *make whole*. *Jehovah-Rapha* doesn't heal half-way. He makes us whole in every area. That concept is difficult for many to comprehend. Healing is often for physical ailments, but it also incorporates wellness of the entire person—body, soul, spirit. David said, "The Lord . . . gathers together the outcasts of Israel. He heals the brokenhearted and binds up their wounds" (Ps. 147:2–3). He's the consummate Healer—of water, land, nations, broken hearts, sicknesses, wounds, and much more. Sickness and sin are linked in the Old Testament (see Ps. 103:2–3); but in the New Testament, the foremost healing is from sin.

Isaiah prophesied that the Messiah would be "wounded for our transgressions . . . bruised for our iniquities; the chastisement for our peace was upon Him, and by His stripes we are healed" (Isa. 53:5). This list covers sin, peace, sorrow, physical wellness, and mental health. Peter quoted Isaiah but with a significant change. Instead of using present tense *are healed*, he used past tense *were healed* (see 1 Pet. 2:24). Because of Jesus' finished work on the whipping post and at the cross, issues which could crop up were already taken care of. We just claim healing. The Greek word which parallels the Hebrew for *healed* is *iaomai*,[123] which includes "personal wholeness—mental, psychological, physical, and spiritual— [and it] flows from [our] conversion."[124]

PART THREE | GLORY PURPOSES

THE HEALER

My brother bought land in Texas and built a small ranch there. One of his plans was to pump water into a creek where wild animals could drink. When I accompanied him to the ranch one day, he received a call from an agency that had tested the ranch's water. Salt levels rendered it unfit for animals. My brother was crushed because that was a main reason he'd purchased the property. As we drove from the ranch back to San Antonio, I prayed with my brother and gave the situation to *Jehovah-Rapha* like Moses had done at Marah when he'd counted on water that turned out to be poison. As we prayed, peace settled over our car. Before we arrived at his house, another company called to suggest an alternate possibility for the water's purification. After later reassessments, he was told that animals could safely drink, and he needed only a water softener for it to be safe for people. That's *Jehovah-Rapha!*

I've also seen *Jehovah Rapha* heal many physical needs. During my *higher* journey, Wade hurt his knee and had difficulty walking because of pain. One morning I shopped for groceries, a job he usually did. While I was gone, Holy Spirit whispered to him about how to get victory. When I returned an hour later, he bounded from the house and headed for the car to help tote groceries. Though I protested, he continued to walk at a normal gait. He told me that after God's prompting, his knee was fine, just in the hour I'd been gone. That's *higher*.

INFUSION

Years ago, Holy Spirit spoke something powerful that has come to be a large part of my ministry. It began when I had dreams and received prophetic words from others telling me healing was in my hands. I soon saw that come to pass. Heat invaded my hands as I prayed for others. People have told me they couldn't continue holding my hands because they were too hot. Then a new phase of this anointing happened. Holy Spirit told me He would use me as an extension cord between Him and others' needs. That came to pass. As I've prayed for people, power has gone down my arms, through my hands, and into others. I compare that happening to when Jesus told the woman with the issue of blood that virtue had gone from Him (see Lk. 8:43–46).

As I've held people's hands or laid mine on them, they've experienced various sensations—shock, tingling, intense heat. When that happens, I first sense a vibration traveling down my arms and into my hands. I feel power transferred into the other person. During this higher journey, an experience with this gift was unusual. In a Monday night class, people gathered around to pray for my back. As others finished, one lady took my hands. For the first time, infusing power went *into* my arms instead of *from* them. I'd never witnessed anyone else operate this way in healing gifts. Holy Spirit did a work in my back that night. Though I was usually a conduit into others, that time, I was the recipient of that mighty power. I was healed.

JEHOVAH-SHAMMAH—THE LORD IS PRESENT

In the Bible, *Jehovah* demonstrated another aspect of His character—He is present. From the beginning, man was created to enjoy God's presence and for God to enjoy man's too. His relationship with Adam and Eve was built on fellowship. God walked with them in the Garden, and they took pleasure in each other's presence (see Gen. 3:8). He later dwelt in a fire, cloud, tabernacle, and temple. In the New Testament, Immanuel is the name most closely associated with *Shammah*. Even before He was born, Jesus was called "Immanuel" meaning "God with us" (Matt. 1:23). This Man was God in a human body, walking among those with whom Father longed to be. Near the end of Ezekiel's book, God assured him that a time of restoration would come when the name of Jerusalem would be "THE LORD IS THERE" (Ezek. 48:35). We are the fulfillment of that prophecy because the Lord dwells inside of us!

Although He lives in us after we're saved, He's also around us because He's omnipresent and omniscient. We can enter His presence and be with Him because the veil was torn in the Holy of Holies (see 1 Cor. 3:16). Through worship, *Shammah* draws close. Angels who are around His throne bring *His* presence into *our* presence. When those heavenly emissaries arrive, our bodies tingle as signs, wonders, and revelations are initiated because "In [His] presence is fullness of joy; at [His] right hand are pleasures forevermore" (Ps. 16:11). His presence is our most valuable resource. We neglect this crucial asset when we don't come into His presence regularly and live to be close with Him. The glory arrives so we can commune together.

MOSES

Moses understood about God's presence. Israel had been in the desert at Sinai for about a year.[125] God told Moses to leave and promised He'd drive out the land's inhabitants from before the Hebrews. However, God said He wouldn't go into their midst because they were "a stiff-necked people" (Exod. 33:3). As a result, people humbled themselves and experienced a great occurrence. Moses pitched a tent away from the camp and called it the "tabernacle of meeting" (Exod. 33:7) where God's presence would reside and Moses would receive direction. There, God's presence was thick, and He spoke to Moses as a "friend" (Exod. 33:11). *Friend* is *re'a*, a "companion . . . [but also] a familiar person . . . [to] associate with."[126] *Jehovah Shammah* wants us to be His devoted friend, not a distant acquaintance.

Moses reminded God that He had told him to bring the people into the Promised Land. He questioned who would go with them; and God responded that His "Presence will go with [them], and [He] will give [them] rest" (Exod. 33:14). Moses said that if God's presence didn't go, he didn't want to leave (see Exod. 33:12–15). His obsession with the Lord's presence served him well. What relationship do you have with God? He desires not only to be your Father but also to have friendship, intimacy, familiarity, and close association with you. Billy Graham said, "Most of us know about God, but that is quite different from knowing God."[127] When we truly know Him as Father and Friend, we will entrust everything to Him.

A friend who knows the Lord intimately told me that everywhere she's lived or worked, she anointed those places as soon as she arrived. She begins each morning in His presence, so whatever happens is filtered through *Shammah*. Once a rattlesnake was found in her employee's work cubicle. She had unknowingly stepped over it all morning. Although the snake looked alive and well, its head was flat like someone or something was standing on it. When authorities removed the snake, the head was no longer flat. My friend said she's sure an angel, *Shammah's* representative, was standing on the head to protect her co-worker. The angelic presence changed a potentially terrible situation.

My sister Liz tells about missionaries working in a Third-World country. One night, a group of twelve people at a church in America felt led to pray for those missionaries. While they interceded, the missionaries across the world went into town to get supplies and traveled back to their camp unharmed. The next day a native man confessed that he and others had followed them. They would've robbed and killed them if the twelve guards hadn't been surrounding them. Imagine. For each prayer warrior, an angel had an assignment—the missionaries' safety. *Jehovah Shammah* sends His representatives because He longs to be with us, protect us, and take care of all our needs.

JEHOVAH-SHALOM—THE LORD OUR PEACE

Gideon

God's character of peace is *Jehovah-Shalom*. When He first showed this attribute, Gideon had been tapped to defeat the Midianites. Before Gideon began his assignment, he sacrificed to the Angel of God. After the Angel touched the meat and bread, fire rose from the rock and consumed the sacrifice. After the Angel spoke to Gideon then disappeared, Gideon realized he'd seen the Angel of the Lord face-to-face (see Judg. 6:1–22). An insecure man, he couldn't fulfill his calling by himself. Many of God's generals completed their commissions despite timidities and perceived inadequacies.

After this encounter, his confidence rose as well as his peace. When Jesus comes on the scene, things change. Gideon constructed an "altar there to the Lord [*Jehovah*] and called it The-Lord-Is-Peace" (Judg. 6:24). The King James Version says he "called it *Jehovahshalom*." That name, *Yehovah Shalowm*, means "*Jehovah* (IS) peace."[128] Again, the redemptive name indicates He not only *brings* peace, but His very character *IS* peace. Resting in Him brings utter peace. Jesus often told followers not to fear. As a matter of fact, the Bible says not to fear 365 times. That's once a day. Peace is one of the fruits of Holy Spirit, so peace belongs to believers (see Gal. 5:22–23). Dwell in the peace that's yours through *Jehovah Shalom*.

PEACE

The English concept of *peace* differs from the Hebrew. In English, the implication is absence of conflict or worry. In Hebrew it's considered being fulfilled. We don't have to succumb to fear of sickness, poverty, danger, or anything else when *Jehovah-Shalom* fulfills His brand of peace. The Lord has thoughts for our good including peace (see Jer. 29:11). When an insurmountable battle looms, "our eyes [must remain] upon [the Lord]" (2 Chron. 20:12), who brings peace as He gives assurances that He's there to deliver us from whatever we encounter. If we trust God and keep our minds on Him, He gives "perfect peace" (Isa. 26:3).

I can relate to this redemptive name of God because that glory manifestation of intense peace comes frequently during worship. When that happens, peace dive-bombs us. Those times are more than feeling serene. Intense peace enters and makes moving arms and legs difficult. One morning an overwhelming peace came over us during worship. When we were finished, I saw a vision of a *Greater Than* sign. Peace that comes from worship is overwhelming, greater-than peace, peace. A heavy blanket drops on us so consummately that Wade has fallen asleep more than once. Before I experienced total peace, I wondered how Jesus' Inner Circle could have been involved in the extreme glory at the Transfiguration and reacted by feeling sleepy (see Lk. 9:28–36). I believe they were experiencing that glory manifestation of utter peace from *Jehovah Shalom*. Sitting and soaking in the glory changes us and our circumstances.

Several years ago, I was near death and taken to the hospital. I needed two units of blood that night and five more before everything was finished. Before discovering my spleen had failed, doctors performed a battery of tests for ten days to find the source of blood loss. They transferred me to a larger hospital for a splenectomy. I settled in that night nervous about surgery the next morning and frazzled by the nearly two weeks of tests and physical weakness. In the middle of the night, a nurse I hadn't seen before nor after stood by my bed. She was different from the others.

"You're gonna be all right," she said.

As her smile exuded peace, the Lord's presence surrounded me. I fell asleep without worrying about the procedure. In the morning before surgery, family members arrived. I told them about the nurse and said she was an angel God had sent. I wasn't afraid. *Jehovah-Shalom* had used a heavenly emissary to bring perfect peace. During one of the hardest ordeals of my life, *Jehovah-Shalom's* peace had dive-bombed me as He took care of everything.

I AM THAT I AM

Many believe Old Testament glory occurrences don't happen today, but that's inaccurate. *Jireh*, *Rapha*, and all other redemptive names are still part of our inheritance. He is I AM, a present-tense God. Moses had such relationship with the Father that he saw many signs and wonders—shoes and clothes didn't wear out in forty years, food rained from heaven (see Deut. 29:5; Exod. 16:4). During the wilderness journey those were *now* needs. They couldn't rely on past experiences or their future in the Promised Land. God supplied necessities freely each time they were needed.

When God first told him about his calling, Moses, like Gideon, was uncertain and insecure. He asked how He should describe the God who was sending Him. The Lord answered, "I AM WHO I AM" (Exod. 3:13-14). Later, He told Moses to "say to the children of Israel: 'The Lord God of your fathers, the God of Abraham, the God of Isaac, and the God of Jacob, has sent me to you. This is My name forever, and this is My memorial to all generations'" (Exod. 3:15). In essence, generations before and after had known and would know I AM.

I love this I AM aspect of God. He's always existed (the memorial), but He's also the God of now and will forever be (His name forever). He's constantly near His people when they need Him. As a matter of fact, He's inside us. The I AM character of God includes other redemptive names. We may have history with God, but we need to forge a NOW relationship with Him as a crucial aspect of our journey. All His promises are for NOW!

JESUS

I AM wasn't just an Old Testament concept. That character was personified by Jesus, who said, "I am the light of the world" (Jn. 8:12) and "before Abraham was, I AM" (Jn. 8:58). He called Himself many different I AM's—the bread of life who satisfies our hunger and thirst; the resurrection and life; the way, truth, and life, and only way to the Father; true vine, door, and good shepherd (see Jn. 6:35; 11:25; 14:6; 15:1; 10:7, 11). He came to earth as the consummate example of I AM to renew God's relationship with man. He assumed the role of a man to meet our needs including salvation. His sacrifice was crucial to those who walked with Him, and He's essential today and forever. He's what we need NOW. Because the Trinity dwells in Christians, They know us intimately and are "our refuge and strength, a very present help in trouble" (Ps. 46:1). They're the I AM. That knowledge comes as we gain intimacy with the Lord in our higher walk. He was, He will be, He is the I AM.

CHAPTER TEN
Prophetic Actions

At the church I attended when I was young, a large portion of some services was dedicated to waiting on Holy Spirit until He revealed a path to victory for a pressing need. For breakthroughs, we had Jericho marches inside the church and around the property. Multiple times, I witnessed healings initiated by an elderly lady blowing on someone. I've seen the church body move together as one got a puzzle piece, then another, then another until the whole picture emerged. From those revelations, Holy Spirit showed us how to break through the enemy's barrier or crisis he had planned. I've witnessed how these disclosures work and later heard a phrase that named them.

I've mentioned these in previous chapters—*prophetic actions*. Often healings, miracles, and breakthroughs come from the revelation God discloses. They're about obeying the Lord's way of delivering results, a *rhema*. Many times God told Moses to use peculiar enactments to make His will happen—extending his hand, striking a rock, putting blood on the doorpost (see Exod. 14:21; 17:6; 12:22). When Israel and Amalek were fighting an intense battle, Moses raised his hands and Israel prevailed. When he lowered them, Amalek triumphed. After someone brought a stone for Moses to sit on, Aaron and Hur supported his arms so those powerful weapons could remain steady and upright until the sun set. The army was victorious over Amalek (see Exod. 17:10–13).

The Word includes many of these prophetic exchanges from God to man. We can emulate how through revelations of prophetic actions, biblical saints maneuvered through a maze of trials. Those examples caused impressive results—cities falling to the ground, the sun standing still, seas rolling back, leprosy vanishing (see Josh. 6:20, 10:13; Exod. 14:21; 2 Ki. 5:14). They were God's intended results initiated by a revelation which someone heard and obeyed. Like those in the Bible, our daily lives are filled with issues and crises for which we need God's guidance. Prophetic actions are a key assuring victory.

WHAT ARE THEY?

Those "weird ways" direct us about how to usher in the glory with signs and wonders following. My mother used to call them God's M.O., His Method of Operation. Prophetic actions are His way of telling us the path for the miraculous to occur, but those instructions are rarely how we might do it. Sometimes, directives are downright strange, but these actions have two common traits. First, revelation comes, maybe as a vision, unction, dream, etcetera. The second aspect for victory is obedience to the revelation. That may mean getting up from our warm, comfy beds; falling on our faces; throwing imaginary weights from our shoulders; or proclaiming specific biblical promises. We receive His timing and His way, then proceed. If we cherish those treasures and act on them, we not only get results for the current need, but God will entrust us with future revelations. If not, He may go elsewhere the next time He has a word about the method which will provide victory. God is constantly disclosing His plans to His kids, but those revelations require responsibility. If the Lord tells us to march, twirl, or be silent but we don't, victory will evade us.

One day a lady phoned for prayer. Because her call came during a time when the Indiana governor had asked for limited physical contact with others, I couldn't go to her house or her come to ours for prayer. Instead, I took the phone to Wade's basement office, and we prayed for her together on the speaker. While Wade led the prayer, I saw a vision of my shaking something above her head. After Wade finished, I shared what I'd seen.

"I saw myself doing a prophetic action." When I told her what I'd seen, she readily agreed. She'd had plenty of exposure to prophetic actions and their results.

I carried my phone upstairs to the living room where maracas sat on the piano. As I reached for them, an angelic presence entered the room.

"I feel . . . ."

Before I could finish my statement, she interrupted. "I feel it, too."

With her in her home across town and me in my house, I shook the brightly colored instruments above the phone while I prayed. His presence was so strong I could barely stand. After the burden lifted, I told her about the presence at my house. Again, she interrupted.

"I know," she said. "I felt Holy Spirit here, too. As you shook the maracas, heat started in the top of my head and went through my body." As a result of my obeying Holy Spirit's direction and my friend's compliance, the Lord answered. We may not understand why something as foolish as shaking a rattle above the phone can accomplish healing across the miles, but it can and does.

Another time, I was in Europe with a group of ladies ministering in churches. We'd gotten up early that morning to fly from Ireland to Italy. The night service would be my turn to preach, and I had my sermon ready—until I boarded the plane. Holy Spirit let me know that what I'd planned needed to be changed. "Breakthrough" came into my spirit.

In our hotel lobby, I prepared my sermon by digging into the Word and praying, but that wasn't enough. I was glad when the hotel clerk let us into our room so I could worship and engage in a powerful breakthrough tool—travail. As I cried out with sobs of travail, Holy Spirit put a prophetic action on my heart. I was to burst balloons to symbolize breakthrough. However, finding balloons was impossible. Being in a foreign country, I had no access to Walmart or anywhere else that sold balloons, but my inability meant nothing where God's ability was concerned.

When we arrived at church, we sat in the second row on a wooden bench. Almost immediately, a lady sat down across the aisle from us. She put three inflated balloons on the seat beside her! My mouth dropped open in disbelief for a second before it turned into a huge smile. I was amazed that again God had not only revealed His M.O. but made it possible to obey. When I approached her and asked if I could have the balloons, she readily agreed. That service was one of the most powerful I've been in, especially when people burst those balloons one at a time. Breakthrough happened in many ways that night. Prophetic actions are a tremendous weapon the enemy can't combat because they're straight from the throne of God.

ILLUSTRATED PROPHECIES

Many biblical prophets illustrated God's word with actions. The book of Hosea is one of those illustrated prophecies. God instructed the prophet to take a prostitute as a wife to parallel Israel's unfaithfulness in taking other loves besides Him (see Hos. 1:2). Another example of an illustrated prophecy was after King Solomon allowed heathen wives to lure him into worshipping other gods. God sent a prophet, Ahijah, to Solomon's servant, Jeroboam. Ahijah took his garment and tore it into twelve pieces. He gave ten to Jeroboam, but the other two pieces he reserved for David's ancestors (see 1 Ki. 11:29–32). This prophetic action demonstrated how God was going to strip the bulk of Solomon's kingdom from his son and give it to Jeroboam. He would keep two tribes for Rehoboam, Solomon's son. It happened just that way.

Ezekiel gave several illustrated prophecies. The Lord told him to lie on his left side and take Israel's sins upon himself. The number of days he lay on his side would be the number of times he'd bear their iniquity—390 days for Israel on his left and forty days for Judah on his right side (see 4:4–6). Another time he was to use a razor on his hair and beard and then divide the cut hair into three piles. One stack Ezekiel was to burn, another to strike with a sword, and a third to throw into the wind. He was also to take a small amount and put it in his garment to represent the faithful remnant that remained (see 5:1–4). These actions denoted fates of Israel. Prophets understood the power that came through obeying God's direction through a prophetic action.

HEALINGS THROUGH PROPHETIC ACTIONS

Miracles transpire as we obey God's guidance through prophetic actions. When I was young, my uncle had been forced to retire from his position in the fire department because of a back injury that severely limited mobility and necessitated his wearing a brace. Though my family had little experience with Holy Spirit, they knew God was a Healer. My parents accompanied my Uncle Clyde to an A.A. Allen service where he was determined to get his miracle.

When Brother Allen called for people to come forward to the prayer line in that big-top tent, Uncle Clyde struggled to make his way to the platform and stand in the line filled with others who were desperate for healing. Though long-term standing was excruciating, he continued to edge forward as each person went away with his or her answer after the preacher laid his hands on them and prayed. When my uncle finally reached the minister who was touted as, "God's man of faith and power," the man of God paused a moment. My uncle didn't know that God was speaking to Reverend Allen about how this miracle would come to fruition.

Brother Allen looked into my uncle's eyes and said, "Are you ready for your miracle?" Uncle Clyde nodded. "Will you obey Holy Spirit?" My uncle nodded again, not quite sure what that meant or what the preacher would say next. He noticed a tent worker bringing a tool box toward him.

"Brother," Pastor Allen said with the authority that comes when God deposits a *rhema* into a person. "Grab this box."

My uncle hesitated. He probably felt like Naaman when he was told to dip in the dirty Jordan River or the Hebrews when Joshua said to march around Jericho in that blistering, desert heat (see 2 Ki. 5:10–12; Josh. 6:6–7). God performs the impossible with methods beyond logic or familiarity. My uncle's back had prevented his carrying heavy objects, but he trusted the word of God through the man of God. With a brief pause, he reached for that heavy toolbox. As his fingers clutched the handle, he wasn't sure if doing what the preacher asked would help or hurt. Would his back even allow him to perform such a grueling task? It did. He picked up the weighty box.

Then Brother Allen issued another order: Carry it around the tent's edge. Obediently, Uncle Clyde gingerly left the make-shift platform and shuffled down the ramp, each step laborious and challenging at first! Then his steps became faster and stronger, and he was free from pain. By the time he'd circled the entire tent, he was nearly running. Amid the crowd's boisterous roar, he set down the toolbox, took off his brace, and walked across the stage twirling it on his cane. Something as silly as a toolbox and our obedience can be God's way of working a miracle.

FINANCES

During a midweek service at the church we attend, Holy Spirit revealed a prophetic action that culminated in provision. After worship, Pastor prayed over the offering. When an usher approached, Holy Spirit began dealing with me: Pastor also needed to receive a prove-me offering. It was a communion service, so I sat impatiently during the sermon and communion meal while I worked up courage to do something beyond my comfort zone. When Pastor began to dismiss, I stood quickly so I wouldn't miss my opportunity. I told the congregation that as a prophetic action to release financial blessing, we should take an offering forward and lay it on the table where communion emblems had sat. I'd sing a song I'd composed about giving, based on Malachi 3:10–12. While I sang the song a second time, the congregation should take offerings forward.

Prophetic Actions

People looked at me quizzically, so I sang with my eyes closed. Despite my discomfort at sharing something most people thought was weird, I knew those peculiar-but-wonderful prophetic actions accomplish much. When I opened my eyes, others were getting out offerings. As I started the second round of the song, we took them forward. After we finished, Pastor prayed dismissal, and folks filed from the church. I'd driven a short distance when Holy Spirit impressed something on me. I'd given from our joint account but not our ministry account. Unlike my usual practice, that night I'd carried both checkbooks in my purse. I had to go back.

Some remained in the building for after-church chatting as I approached Pastor and gave him the other check. I left that night knowing I'd obeyed, even to do what many people likely thought was utter idiocy. I don't know what happened to others because of their prove-me offerings, but I know about us. That event led to multiple financial blessings for both the Urbans and Restoration Ministries. When God has you prove Him His way, circumstances change.

Another prophetic action brought about financial blessing to a dynamic Christian couple. He was a struggling truck driver, experiencing such money problems that his wife had yard sales to supplement their income. Holy Spirit moved on Wade to do a prophetic action. As the husband held out his hands, Wade slapped them to activate a blessing for a million-dollar idea. As both their hands stung from that action, they knew something happened in the heavens. Before a year was over, he'd gotten hauling contracts for more than a million dollars. Prophetic actions, combined with obedience, bring realities from Heaven into this earthly realm.

CHAPTER ELEVEN
Reasons for the Glory: Other Purposes

Besides demonstrating aspects of His redemptive names, the glory comes for other reasons. It may show up to validate God's generals (see Exod. 33:17–19) like God proved His Son with glory manifestations. When Jesus was baptized by John the Baptist, the heavens opened, and Holy Spirit descended on Jesus as a dove (see Matt. 3:14–16). The writer of Hebrews alludes to when Jesus spoke of salvation; God confirmed His words to those around with signs, wonders, miracles, and Holy Spirit manifestations (see Heb. 2:3–4). The glory came at Jesus' birth as a multitude of angels announced His arrival to shepherds on the hillsides (see Lk. 2:9–13). Later, a mass of heavenly hosts joined the shepherds as they rejoiced about the Savior's birth (see Lk. 2:13–14). The glory is an incredible facet of our Christian walk and presents itself for many others purposes.

VALIDATION OF OUR GIFTS

The Transfiguration

One magnificent, powerful glory event was the Transfiguration. Before that mountaintop experience, disciples had known Jesus as a man. There they witnessed His deity. Moses, Elijah, and Jesus' Inner Circle (Peter, James, and John) were with Jesus on the mountain for that occurrence. *Transfigured* is *metamorphoo*, to "change . . . transform,"[129] and that's just what happened. Jesus' face glowed like the sun, and His clothes shone white like light (see Matt. 17:2). This description reminds me of Moses in God's presence when God's glory shone so brightly, Moses had to wear a veil (see Exod. 34:33). However shining faces aren't the only way we can be transformed. Paul says

Reasons for the Glory: Other Purposes

that rather than seeking confirmation of others, we should "be transformed by the renewing of [our minds]" (see Rom. 12:2). That use of *transform* is also *metamorphoo*. Like Jesus was transformed in His body, we can also be transformed in our minds.

The Transfiguration on the mountain had many purposes. This scene was part of God's acknowledgment of His Son's upcoming ordeal. Moses, Elijah, and Jesus "spoke of His decease which He was about to accomplish at Jerusalem" (Lk. 9:31). When Peter suggested making three tabernacles, God again validated Jesus as His voice boomed from the brilliant cloud overshadowing them: "This is My beloved Son, in whom I am well pleased. Hear Him!" (Matt. 17:5). As Jesus first began His ministry, God had also spoken words of validation for Jesus (see Lk. 3:21-22). Now Father stressed that they should, "Hear Him." Scarce, precious time was left for Jesus' companions to hear all He had to say and pass it along to those not only who remained but also to other generations forever!

As God's thunderous voice spoke, disciples were afraid (see Matt. 17:4-6). Like God warned Ezekiel of his potential for emotional reactions to rejection, Jesus comforted His disciples by saying, "Arise, and do not be afraid" (Matt. 17:7). How like our Lord to understand human feelings and give encouragement! Luke's version adds another facet. He says the voice came *from* the cloud, and they were "fearful as they entered the cloud" (Lk. 9:34-35). That cloud was God's glory. As we see phenomena like glory clouds, we may respond in different ways. Marvelous occurrences bring awe but still a part of us is leery, even fearful, like the disciples.

Mark stated that before this event, Jesus had said "some standing [there would] not taste death till they see the kingdom of God present with power" (Mk. 9:1). That could have been a reference to the arrival of Holy Spirit, but Jesus may also have been indicating what would happen about a week later at the Transfiguration. After Jesus' resurrection, disciples alluded to this occurrence. Peter revealed that this was not a "cunningly devised fable . . . [but rather they] were eyewitnesses of His majesty . . . when such a voice came to Him from the Excellent Glory . . . and [they] heard this voice which came from heaven when [they] were with Him on the holy mountain" (see 2 Pet. 1:16-18). As an eyewitness, he was stressing that this incident hadn't been concocted or exaggerated. In the first chapter of John's gospel, he said they "beheld His glory, the glory as of the only begotten of the Father" (Jn. 1:14). That reference could be about this event. John's later description of the Lord says, "His countenance was like the sun shining in its strength" (Rev. 1:16). This comment undoubtedly refers to the mountain experience with Jesus. These men were forever impacted by this great glory event. Glory events can happen now too.

Clouds

Besides at the Transfiguration, in many biblical stories glory arrived in a cloud. After God's presence, the Ark of the Covenant, was carried into Solomon's temple, glory came in as a thick cloud. Trumpeters and singers were in one accord praising and thanking God. As they lifted their voices with trumpets, cymbals, and other musical instruments, they praised Him. The cloud filled the Lord's house so densely priests couldn't continue ministering (see 2 Chron. 5:13–14).

After His resurrection and promise of Holy Spirit, a cloud took Jesus to Heaven (see Acts 1:9). Both John and Daniel say He'll also return in the clouds (see Rev. 1:7; Dan. 7:13). Jesus told His followers they would see the Son of Man sitting at the right hand of Power and coming on the clouds (see Matt. 26:64). Ezekiel saw a vision of a temple filled with a cloud in the Inner Court. Glory went up from the cherubim who were standing in the temple. The whole house was filled with a cloud of great brightness which accompanied God's glory (see 10:3–4). As our cloud of worship fills our temples, God responds.

Clouds represent His presence, leadership, protection, direction, and judgment.[130] During the trek to the Promised Land, both a cloud and fire directed travel. Whenever the cloud moved, Moses and his group knew they were to journey elsewhere. An angel accompanied the group heading for the Promised Land (see Num. 9:17–18; Exod. 32:34). When Moses received the second tablets, the Lord came in a cloud to give direction and renew their covenant (see Exod. 34:4–10). At times, Moses couldn't enter the tabernacle of meeting because God's presence (*kabod*) rested in a thick cloud (see Exod. 40:34–36). When Moses entered, the cloud stood at the door, and God spoke to him. As Moses demonstrated, we shouldn't take a step unless the Lord leads us.

On the mountain Moses and his elders observed visions of a sapphire street and saw God's glory in a limited way. God sent Moses farther up into a glory cloud for six days. On the seventh, God called to him from a cloud. Moses stayed on the mountain forty days and nights while the Lord imparted revelation. Besides giving the law, He instructed Moses about the important job of setting up the tabernacle (see Exod. 24:9–25:9). Many others in the Bible experienced amazing revelations as a result of God's glory.

REVELATION/DIRECTION

Whether God comes in a cloud or another way, when He reveals His plan, "the steps of a good man are ordered by the Lord, and He delights in his way" (Ps. 37:23). Like Israel discovered, God wants to take us into our Promised Land, our own *higher* journey, but we need to follow His direction. His glory often lingers in one location; but when it moves, we should move with it. We can't become too comfortable where we are because His moves come in seasons—Azusa Street, Faith Healers, Charismatic Renewal, River Movements. All were wonderful and powerful for a time; but when God said to move to the next encampment, people needed to relocate. They couldn't become too complacent by staying instead of growing by going.

Ezekiel's book shows many revelations—the assignment as a watchman, the future of Israel, and the foretelling of Messiah. Others in the Bible heard from God. When Jehoshaphat asked Elisha about an upcoming battle, Elisha sent for a musician. As the musician played, the Lord's hand came on Elisha, who prophesied about a prophetic action that would bring victory (see 2 Ki. 3:15–19). An angel of the Lord gave Philip instructions to leave Samaria and minister to an Ethiopian eunuch (see Acts 8:26). In a vision, an angel told Cornelius to send men to Joppa with a word for Peter (see Acts 10:3–5). This great event opened the door for the Gentiles' salvation. The angel Gabriel approached Mary to tell her God had chosen her (see Lk. 1:26–38). A star appeared and gave guidance to Wise Men for their long journey to the Messiah. Then the star lingered over the child (see Matt. 2:2, 9). Glory events happen today, too. Nearly every class session or in worship at home, the time of adoration of Father ends with revelation.

National/International

Many years ago, Holy Spirit blessed me with an intense revelation gift to hear about and intercede against the enemy's plans for national and international crises. I've received both types of those revelations. The first time, none of us at church that night knew how to proceed. The experience began when something or someone pushed me, and I fell to the floor. This had to be an angel because no one else was near me. I saw a vision with several segments—birds swooping down, people scattering in fear, and the blackest black I'd ever seen. The meaning of that vision was exposed a few days later when 9/11 occurred. By the way, I heard a reporter on the towers' collapse use the very description I'd shared— "the blackest black" he'd ever seen. Future revelations of this type were received with utmost prayer and intercession.

Since then, I've had other visions with an urgency like this one. After we acted upon those revelations, we've found out how God had thwarted the enemy's plans. The visions come when an angelic presence pervades the room, and a strong heaviness and life-death feeling engulfs me. I'm unable to stand; even sitting, I go limp. I can't lift my head, limbs, or fingers. Then I see a series of visions which eventually add up to God's warning. As soon as I can move, I write them down and share them. We talk it over in body ministry until we have direction for how to pray. We go to the Lord in intense intercession and have experienced amazing results.

The Palm

Often, my husband and I sit in God's presence to seek His will. *Jehovah-Shammah* has given direction for everything from what to preach at an upcoming service to where we should sow an offering. I've personally witnessed multiple glory events which happened for a variety of purposes. During my *higher* journey, beginning with the first song in our home worship one night, I cried in His intense presence. After three songs, I moved from the piano to a chair and soaked in the heavy *kabod*. Suddenly, a tap on my chair startled me. I looked to see if our cat was climbing up the side of my chair, but I was alone except for my heavenly visitor. I saw a vision:

> *An angel stood with a golden lyre. Adorning each of the top corners were golden, ornate shapes I didn't recognize. He held the instrument but didn't play it. I saw one word: "GO!"*

I wasn't sure where we were to go or what we were to do, but I knew God was giving direction and a commission. God would tell us when our seasons changed. Our job would be to listen and obey. When He clarified His will, we would be like Abraham. We'd saddle our donkey and leave in the morning. Though I didn't understand all of the vision, it soon made sense and gave clear instructions about matters for which we'd sought answers from the Lord.

This vision grew clearer when I read Ezekiel's description of the temple. He mentioned palm trees on the corners of gateposts and other places. One description said palms and cherubim were carved on temple windows and archways (see Ezek. 40:22, for example). Solomon's temple, which housed His glory, also had palm trees.[131] I realized that what I had seen on the lyre in my vision were probably palm trees and were related to my *higher* journey, especially to worship. As Jesus rode into Jerusalem on Palm Sunday, people waved and spread palm branches and clothes on the road and accompanied Him (see Jn. 12:13; Mk. 11:8-9). Those branches were like our worship. We crave and celebrate *His* presence in *our* presence. The palm tree has much to say.

A palm represents many things. Though other trees may grow crooked or misshapen, palms are upright. This speaks of how our character should be—tall and erect as people of integrity. We don't sway when it's convenient for us or when others twist what's right to suit a personal agenda. A palm is also fruitful with dates—a nutritious, life-sustaining food. We should not only bear good fruit ourselves but should judge the good or bad fruit others bear. The palm has elasticity, and its fiber's consistency allows upward growth no matter what weighs it down. We Christians may go through trials that are heavy burdens, but we should continue growing toward Father. Finally, a palm tree is beautiful as it's framed by the sky. God wants us to be lovely about and to others.[132] We should practice: "Whatever things are true ... noble ... just ... pure ... lovely ... of good report, if there is ... virtue and ... anything praiseworthy—meditate on these things" (Phil. 4:8). I love this list! We don't become immersed in ugliness around us if we meditate on His beauty. My vision not only gave direction to "Go!" but also how I should act. This tree's lessons can propel us higher.

Restructure

Through mine and others' dreams and visions, Holy Spirit gave more direction about how Wade and I should proceed. A friend dreamed I'd been receiving words of knowledge and handing them off to others. The next night, I had a dream with a similar message. A few days later, one of my sisters dreamed I needed to work on our house's foundation. Then, another sister had a dream—Four dreams in a few days. I understood the essence of God's message, but I wasn't certain about some interpretations. Three of my sisters and I met on Zoom, and we talked until we understood God's communication. As each sister—Lynda, Becky, Anita—contributed her insight, a picture formed. Basically, Holy Spirit was saying that aspects of our ministry needed to be restructured.

Because of Wade's anointing to preach, over the years I'd evolved into a Martha. Wade and I were always a team; but whenever Holy Spirit showed me something, I often deferred to Wade to follow through with the revelation. As my friend's dream indicated, I literally handed off words of knowledge for Wade to share and pray over instead of acting on my own revelations in a Mary role. I should've stayed at Jesus' feet and shared His revelations myself. Holy Spirit was calling me to operate in my own anointing, and my path to *higher* had to include taking ownership of what He gave. That aspect of our ministry foundation needed to change, and it demanded I extend my tent pegs from where they'd been planted for a long time (see Isa. 54:2–3). I didn't understand other details of ministry foundations that needed to change, but I knew they'd be part of going higher. Watching results unfold would be a wonderful element in this journey's beauty.

Results

I heard, took restructuring messages seriously, and stepped out. Consequently, Wade and I saw added miracles and abundant revelations. I had increased anointing, confidence, and authority during classes and services and moved without interrupting Holy Spirit's flow. I also operated in the Spirit in ways I hadn't for a long time or maybe forever. For example, one Sunday, I gave a message in tongues with the interpretation, something I hadn't done for many years.

Another time Wade and I were ministering at an Indiana church. A lady in my prayer line told me her need. As I began to pray, I saw a name flash in a vision. When I asked her if that meant anything to her, she began to sniffle.

"I babysit for a girl with that name," she answered. "She's been sick." By that revelation the Lord had told her He knew both her and that child intimately.

The same thing happened as I ministered in Arizona. After I laid my hands on a young girl, she was slain in the Spirit. As she lay on the floor, I continued to pray, and again a name flashed in a vision. I hesitated to share the old-fashioned name I hadn't heard in a long time, but I asked her mother if they knew anyone with that name. She said no, but her daughter tapped my shoulder later as I finished praying for someone else. When she'd gotten up from the floor, her mother had asked her about the name. As it turned out, that was her best friend's middle name. That revelation said that God not only knew that girl well but loved her and her friend. Those revelations came as a result of *higher*, as I stepped up and out like I should have been doing all along.

House

During this time period, Holy Spirit gave more personal direction for Wade and me. One evening while sitting in His presence, I saw another vision:

> Two houses were sitting side-by-side with connecting roofs. The one on the left had a glass roof; the other, a regular shingled one. Water had come down on the glass roof and onto the attached valley between the roofs with nowhere for it to go.

Normally, a roof in a dream represents protection and covering. In addition, a glass roof can symbolize that the dreamer has received part of the message but will gather more information. It also represents prosperity, new openings, and attention to things around you.[133] All those symbols would fit with what ultimately became evident to us.

I discovered from this and other visions that the Lord was giving direction for relocating, though at the time we weren't sure where. In later months my friend again dreamed that Wade and I were having a celebration gathering. Our house was constructed of two houses with some decorations that were out-of-style, and some were updated. The smaller house was the foyer for the larger one. This dream made sense about a month after the angel had shown me, "GO!"

For years, Wade and I had known we'd eventually relocate. We had looked at houses in different cities and states. One day during this higher journey, we looked at one in Ohio. We hadn't intended to make an offer; but after we saw it, the house was what we wanted. That night we prayed together and asked Holy Spirit to give a dream with a yes or no. He did. In the dream, we were in the town where we'd looked at the house. I was taking care of a baby I adored. As we discussed it the next morning, we felt God was saying to go forward with the purchase.

As each step in the buying process brought doubts, God reinforced our purchase decision with visions, dreams, scriptures, and other confirmations. In one dream we had twin babies, and again I adored them. We felt the Lord was saying we'd keep our Indiana ministry, but He was going to give a second assignment in Ohio. That home we ultimately bought had many aspects from my friend's dream and was close to my childhood house, part of my first dream that started this higher journey. For a time, we literally had two houses—Two ministries, two roofs. Also, the new house was a condo with a roof touching the adjoining unit. Spiritually, we still believe there will be a second ministry that will give rain (Holy Spirit) on the roof an outlet from which to flow.

TO TAKE PEOPLE HOME

Another reason for God's glory is to usher His kids to their heavenly homes. The Psalmist says, "Precious in the sight of the Lord is the death of His saints" (Ps. 116:15). When Christians pass away, Heaven doesn't count it as a sorrowful occasion but a celebration. When the time comes, the Lord personally rejoices to have His children with Him in Heaven. I once saw an online post showing a patient being airlifted, but he or she died as the helicopter rose. At the time of death, a flash of lightning shot up from the helicopter. That's a perfect picture of Heaven's fireworks when a Christian goes home.

When Jesus died and again at the resurrection, Heaven responded with manifestations. Darkness came at noon; the curtain in the Holy of Holies was torn from top to bottom; an earthquake occurred; rocks split; graves opened; and the dead were raised and walked around the city. After His resurrection, angels with a countenance like lightning were at the tomb in snow-white garments (see Matt. 27:45–53; 28:2–3). Those glory occurrences celebrated His home-going.

Tony

I've witnessed this phenomenon of God's welcoming His kids home through glory events. My brother-in-law Tony was a man who wholeheartedly loved God. About ten years ago, he and my sister Anita snapped pictures of a rainbow cradling their home. A week later, another rainbow appeared, but the end went into their garage (see Appendix #7). They were amazed at that lovely sight which represented God's love and promises. Just like Ezekiel received a message when he saw rainbows, those Arizona rainbows were instrumental in showing my sister and her husband God's beauty even in a terrible situation when Tony was hospitalized for a potential blood clot in his leg. After he was released, his recovery was long, but he grew better and stronger.

Tony finally returned to work and his daily routines on a limited basis. One morning, he kissed Anita goodbye as he went excitedly to the garage to take his first bike ride since before his hospitalization. When he didn't come home as soon as my sister thought he should, she went out to drive around the neighborhood and check on him. There in the garage where that rainbow had ended, she found his body on the floor beside his bike. In the days following his death, a snow overspread the desert terrain. Anita took numerous pictures outside her house to commemorate the unusual happening. Photos showed dozens of orbs surrounding their house (see Appendix #8). I'm certain Tony received a wondrous, heavenly welcome when he passed. Those angels had been assigned to escort God's sweet son, His Tony, home.

Kristi

That celebration also happened with my friend Kristi who'd been diagnosed with advanced cancer before we got to know her. Through her, I witnessed another glory manifestation I'd rarely heard about or seen—angel feathers. Kristi found them everywhere and filled multiple baggies with those wonders. When they appeared to any of us, the feathers were usually tiny, so we weren't sure if we'd gotten them into the bag. They grew inside their container, so eventually some developed into fairly large ones.

The last months before her passing, Kristi had grown more in love with her Savior. After she was comatose in hospice, the hospital staff was surprised she was holding onto life so long. One Sunday after I visited my dear friend who had become another daughter to us, I drove home in sorrow. During the trip back to our house, Holy Spirit gave me a message for when I saw her the next Tuesday. At our Monday night streaming, my mind was preoccupied with that message I was to deliver the next morning: *It's okay to let go.* After the streaming program, I shared God's communication with others who remained at our house. Then angelic beings created a miracle.

A class member had left our house but called because she couldn't find her keys. When she told me where she'd been sitting, I went to the antique pew, lifted the cushion, and gasped. Beneath the pillow lay the biggest angel feather I'd ever seen (see Appendix #9). The lady who later found her keys had called because the Lord wanted me to give Kristi this good-bye/welcome-home gift. The next day, I pinned it to her pillow and told her God's message—*It's okay to let go*. No one would be disappointed with her—not her husband, kids, me, nor especially her dear Father. From her coma, a tear slid down her beautiful face. Within two hours, she was with Jesus.

Her visitation was to be Sunday evening at the church we attend. During the morning service, someone approached me to say his grandson had seen angels around the sanctuary. I snapped pictures and I too saw a multitude of orbs. As with our Tony, angels had come to take God's sweet Kristi home. Like He does with other Christians who finish their earthly journeys, God welcomed His Kristi and Tony home with much rejoicing.

TO GIVE COMMISSIONS

When God sends us on the journey toward destiny, His presence often accompanies that revelation of our purpose. The glory came as Ezekiel received his assignment from God personally to speak judgment to Israel (see 3:4–6), but Ezekiel wasn't the only biblical saint who received his commission through a glory event. Jacob stopped for the night on his way to Haran and had a dream—a ladder that reached heaven with angels ascending and descending (see Gen. 28:10–12). God was giving Jacob his assignment—to birth the nation of Israel with its tribes. Several years later, he experienced another glory event. By that time, eleven of his twelve sons were already born to carry on his legacy. Then he wrestled with the pre-incarnate Christ until He gave him a blessing. The Lord renamed him from Jacob to Israel (see Gen. 32:24–28).

Jacob's descendant Moses had been tending his father-in-law's flock. That seemed to be a paltry job, but God had greater plans for a bigger group of sheep. As Moses took his flock of sheep toward the back of the desert to Mount Horeb, the Angel of the Lord appeared in a glory manifestation when a burning bush wasn't being consumed. God spoke to Moses and gave him his commission—to go before Pharaoh then lead His people out of Egypt (see Exod. 3:1–12). The word *bush* is used to describe not only a plant but also means "to prick."[134] God pricked Moses' heart to pick up the heavy mantle of destiny.

The word *prick* reminds me of Saul's glory experience. As he traveled to persecute Christians, Jesus met him on the Road to Damascus and said it's "hard for [Saul] to kick against the pricks" (Acts 26:14 KJV). Saul of Tarsus had recently witnessed Stephen's poignant speech which included a glory event where Stephen's face resembled an angel. As Stephen looked toward Heaven, he saw God's glory (see Acts 6:15; 7:55). Instead of responding to this anointed event and accepting Stephen's words which proved Jesus as Messiah, Saul consented to his death and later arrested others who believed in Jesus (see Acts 7:58–8:3). When blinded by a light on that road to Damascus, he could truly see what he didn't see before (see Acts 9). He accepted his commission from the Lord and devoted the rest of his days to the One he'd formerly worked so vehemently against. When he personally experienced the glory manifestation, he was changed.

Though a great glory event didn't always happen, many who weren't qualified by the world's standards received commissions through marvelous events. Amos, the shepherd, didn't have an education or fancy job. Though we're not told that a mighty glory event occurred, God gave this unqualified man a message for the king himself (see Amos 1:1; 7:14–15). God told Jeremiah about his being ordained as a prophet before he was conceived. Then God touched his lips (see Jer. 1:4–9). Isaiah, whose mouth wasn't under subjection, received his prophet's commission in a glory event involving seraphim (see Isa. 6:5–7). These and other men had flaws that could disqualify them from ministry. Despite faults, God had a destiny for them all, and He often showed up to give it through a glory event.

Our Commission

One night years ago, angelic presences were so thick that walking through our house was difficult for us. My mother, my own mentor in the supernatural, said maybe God had sent them to bring our commission. That ended up being true. We, too, were the least likely God would use. We both had gone through divorces. We both had made many mistakes when we were younger. Neither of us was seminary-trained. As a woman in ministry, I'm sometimes not accepted because of gender. Our experiences and personalities weren't negative to God and didn't change the destiny He had planned—to preach and teach others, especially about Holy Spirit. Like Ezekiel's life changed forever, ours was transformed, too. Sometimes that was difficult, but the call has given much richness to us as we've traversed this humbling trek, one day, one step at a time.

After my *higher* journey began, Holy Spirit clarified our new assignment. One morning as His presence filled my office during devotions, I read this: "You be watchful in all things, endure afflictions, do the work of an evangelist, fulfill your ministry" (2 Tim. 4:5). I knew the Lord was telling us He would send us in a new evangelism direction. Though I still don't know specifics, it will be a magnificent expedition to pursue that destiny.

Several months later, I had another dream:

> *I was at an awards' ceremony. A man with an accent raised a paper that recorded my contributions or accomplishments for God's Kingdom. As he held it up, I saw a list of several things, but at the bottom was a hole that looked like part of the record had been burned off. I sat in the assembly for a while; then I got impatient. I heard what the speaker was saying about me, but I grew more and more eager to get back to work on things I needed to do for the Lord.*

I woke up and lay there a few seconds when the dream continued as a vision:

> *As I rose to leave the room, the speaker came behind me and said, "Accept your assignment."*

I'm still reflecting on the full meaning of that revelation. I know my desire is, above all, to use the rest of my life to be about Father's business. I assume by the missing section of the list that He's warning me that part of my *higher* journey can be unfulfilled if I don't pursue all He has for my assignment. Between family obligations and other ministry duties, I sometimes grow lax about chasing a new level in the Lord. Was He saying by the list's burned part that I could fritter away an opportunity which I have been brought to earth to accomplish? *Higher* needs to be my passion. I should be single-mindedly eager to pursue the Father's business.

PART FOUR

FROM GLORY TO GLORY

CHAPTER TWELVE
The Story Is Unfolding

TRANSFORMATION

Since I began my journey to *higher* more than three years ago, I've had many higher experiences. I've seen so many incredible events and prayers answered that I can't remember them all. During this time, I progressed toward *higher*, but I wanted it all to happen yesterday. At first, I was disappointed that I wasn't progressing quickly enough. However as time passed, I realized each glory experience had made me a different person. Those changes also happened to many saints who answered their calls to higher—Moses, Peter, Isaiah, etcetera.

In each occurrence, "with unveiled face, beholding as in a mirror the glory of the Lord, [I have been] transformed into the same image from glory to glory, just as by the Spirit of the Lord" (2 Cor. 3:18). As we remove the veil from our faces, we take on more of God's character. Paul used *doxa* when he said that though we may be suffering now, those trials can't compare to the glory that will ensue (see Rom. 8:18). Despite obstacles, transformation has taken place as Holy Spirit revealed characteristics to change. But though I've progressed and have been transformed—*metamorphooed*—I still have a long way to go. As the Lord's glory renews me and the veil comes off, I see more of Him and less of me. It's a blessing, and I am different.

PART FOUR | FROM GLORY TO GLORY

PERSONAL REVELATIONS

For many years, glory experiences have come often during worship at home. Throughout this higher journey, they've been more frequent and intense. One night, sitting in the Lord's presence, I saw an unfolding vision:

> *I was in a classroom with cupboards resembling those in schools when I was a child. They weren't long coat closets but rather had top and bottom cupboards. I saw myself approach and open the first one. Inside was heavy, durable, burnt-orange cookware, similar to what we used in the Sixties. I knew what I needed to do: make a meal for others. Because it was a school, I knew I'd be teaching; but I needed to plan for my students now, using tools I'd learned since childhood.*

The Lord is readying us for His service. I believe the cookware from when I was younger refers to how I learned about Holy Spirit's workings during my childhood. Months later, another vision referred to this message:

> *I saw a huge, old, pot-bellied stove with pans simmering on top.*

I felt Holy Spirit was saying a new assignment was imminent. He was telling me to prepare for when this teaching would begin. However family issues arose, and I didn't spend as much time pursuing *higher*. I missed teaching or even attending some Monday classes. After that happened, I dreamed again to prioritize and put teaching ahead of minutiae and even life crises. I needed to do God's things instead of just good things. A few months later, one of my sisters, Lynda, dreamed about me twice. When that happens, it means "the thing is established by God, and God will shortly bring it to pass" (Gen. 41:32). In one of her dreams:

> *I was going back to work. It was the same job I did as a high school teacher, but it was somehow different from before. I was in a familiar place but with a new focus.*

Another Sunday, Wade and I stayed home from church because of snow already covering the ground and more inches expected. Instead of attending a service online, we worshiped at home. As we did, an intense presence entered so profoundly that opening my eyes was difficult. In that atmosphere, Holy Spirit gave two visions. I understood one meaning, but the other was unclear:

> *I saw a short, green ladder. I wasn't just climbing; I was scurrying up. When I got to the top, I dived into the deep end of a great pool of*

water. The scene changed. I saw a crown which resembled those used in coronations. It had a gold band around the bottom with vertical, golden strips from top to bottom. At the top was a large adornment, and jewels decorated all those vertical gold strips, plus the horizontal gold at the bottom. Between vertical bars was red fabric.

The green on the ladder could have many meanings. One is praise, so Holy Spirit's again telling me that praise and worship will advance me quickly. However green also means other things: prosperity, health, and hope. I received all those promises into my spirit. My diving into the water reminds me of Ezekiel's river. I can't stand on the sides or wade in the shallow parts. I must be completely committed to growing higher in Him. Red refers to Jesus' blood and sacrifice, His deity. I believe the crown is another promise. Like when I talked about receiving His commission, I believe a coronation is getting ready to take place. However I need the Lord to show me when and where. I give myself to His will and timing.

SIGNS AND WONDERS

Signs and wonders have been plentiful during this journey. Years ago, when I studied about Elijah while writing my book, *The Elijah Anointing*, I grew excited about signs and wonders he experienced: translations at will, drought, showdowns with prophets, a deluge of rain, a foot race with a chariot (see 1 Ki. 17:1; 18:40, 45–46). His experiences came as he believed the Lord's promises and took preconceived limits off God. Though I wanted what Elijah had experienced and had made gains, my progress wasn't enough. Despite delays, God has still performed mighty signs and wonders during my time of pursuing *higher*. For example, one man who sought for decades to be filled with Holy Spirit was baptized in the Spirit one night as he visited our house.

During Monday worship before class, the glory came in powerfully and often. Consistently, we witnessed images of orbs in pictures. One night, a photo revealed an angel with yellow hair above where a couple was worshiping (see Appendix #10). Another night one worshiper came in after we'd begun to sing. She smelled an overwhelming fragrance from worship. I also smelled an intense, beautiful fragrance one morning as I did devotions in my office. Worshiping at church another Sunday morning, I began to wave my hands to stir the atmosphere. When I did, the guitarist in front of me said he had to brace himself because a glory wave nearly knocked him down.

Another time we were visiting family and preaching in Arizona. On the drive from Tucson, I saw beams of light from the sun. When we exited the I-10 interstate, we stopped at a gas station. As I stood outside, I snapped pictures of mountain ranges. When I got in the car and looked at the pictures, the distant mountains weren't the story. A beam of light came from the sun and ended at my feet (see Appendix #11). During that trip, God's glory prevailed in many ways.

Wonders of Nature

Another wonder of nature occurred on a previous trip to Arizona. My brother and I were driving from Phoenix to Tucson during monsoon season, and a bad storm was forecast. I don't like to drive in inclement weather, so I gave the weather to the Lord. I reminded Him of another time years before when Wade and I were traveling. Menacing tornado clouds had broken up after I rebuked that storm. Now, years later, storm clouds on the way to Tucson looked foreboding, and rain pelted our car. I rebuked those threatening clouds and told them that God was covering us, so even heavy rain had to stop. The downpour eased up immediately. A couple times when it started again, I repeated, "No!" and it stopped or diminished to a fine mist.

In a few miles, clouds grew darker; but as we rounded a curve, the sight was incredible. Thick, black clouds overspread the upcoming horizon where we were to drive. In front of us, though, beneath the treacherous-looking cloud spanning the landscape, was a sliver of sunlight—right over the interstate where we would drive. I praised the Lord for that miraculous sight! At our exit, another wonder occurred. As we veered onto the ramp and proceeded toward the stop sign at the bottom, my brother pointed to the interstate we'd just left. Cars that continued across the bridge at our exit were being pelted with the storm that had been told by the Master to avoid us. We drove down the hill to the stop sign and on to my brother's house with just a bit of rain. How amazing that life's storms must obey God's voice through our proclamations.

Audible Voices And Sounds

I've rarely heard audible voices though many in the Bible did: Jesus, Saul, Moses, Ezekiel, John, and others (see Matt. 3:17; Acts 9:4; Exod. 3:4; Ezek. 9:1; Rev. 1:10). That experience happened to me one fall as I spoke at an

The Story Is Unfolding

Indiana conference. After we prayed in front of the platform and started toward our seats, someone behind me said, "Connie!" I turned around, but no one was there. I scoured the group; people weren't looking at me as if they had called my name. Later, I again heard, "Connie!" No one standing behind me said she had spoken it. I didn't know how to process this audible-voice experience, so I went on with my sermon. Though I don't know why He spoke aloud, His presence was at that ladies' conference, and I learned a lesson about the glory.

Perhaps I missed an incredible event that was to unfold during that occasion, but I now know that the next time, I should stop and see what He has to say. Not many people wait on the Lord like we used to, and I needed to change that in myself. The voice that day wasn't the last time during my higher journey that I heard my name spoken aloud by someone. Though a lady sitting near me hadn't said my name, I prayed with her, and Holy Spirit gave a prophetic word she needed to hear. A third time I recognized the voice as a desperate friend. Later she and I worshiped on the phone until peace came into her home. Perhaps those audible voices were signs that I will go higher as I listen and heed His call. Times when God speaks aloud are for an important purpose.

Another experience dealt with an audible sound that wasn't a voice. One morning while darkness still prevailed, I was half asleep and half awake. In the hall in front of our bedroom, a phone rang, loud and shrill. Startled, I awoke fully with dread because we have no phone in our hallway. I also knew that when a call comes in the night, it's usually bad news. I prayed intensely and texted siblings, children, stepchildren, and prayer warriors to cover loved ones.

One dark morning about two weeks later, I'd been up a short time when my cellphone rang. My nephew from Texas was calling to tell me my brother was hospitalized. The previous day, not having heard from his dad for a while, he'd contacted authorities and asked for a wellness check. The sheriff found my brother lying on the cabin floor at his ranch. He'd suffered a stroke and had lain in that deserted cabin for three days. The day before my nephew's call, doctors had little hope of survival. By the time he called me, my brother had already begun to show stronger vital signs and some communication. As I write this months later, my brother is living at home and progressing. That tragedy turned into a miracle because Holy Spirit came before us to intercede.

That wasn't the last time a noise woke me. These experiences were part of a higher walk I hadn't encountered before. *Higher* includes willingness to go places or experience events that may seem weird, even to ourselves. Holy Spirit's "weirdness" is the *higher* I've been journeying toward and longing for. Learning to listen to someone calling your name, the phone ringing in the hall, or receiving any warning from God is crucial.

Holy Spirit's Language

Holy Spirit prompted me to set aside time each morning to pray in tongues and intercede as needs arose. At first it seemed like a long time to fit into my busy mornings, but I quickly changed that mindset. I knew that obedience shouldn't be a chore but rather a delight. Paul instructs us to "pray [. . .] always with all prayer and supplication in the Spirit" (Eph. 6:18). Using not only our English to pray and worship but also our prayer language is crucial. Holy Spirit understands what's happening or what the enemy's planning even when we don't (see 1 Cor. 14:15). As we pray with His language, "We do not know what we should pray for as we ought, but the Spirit Himself makes intercession for us with groanings which cannot be uttered" (Rom. 8:26). That principle has been a reality in my life and now during this journey.

One startling example came after I devoted time to prayer language. On the first morning I started my praying-in-tongues regimen, Holy Spirit led me to worship. Then I saw a vision:

> *I was looking out the back door of my sister Anita's Arizona home. A car was parked on the patio. I didn't see the make of the car because I knew the hood ornament was the important item. It was ornate and shaped like a dog. I knew that dog was precious and costly. I looked to my left and saw Anita lumbering down the hallway toward me. Her mannerisms, rumpled nightgown, and untied bathrobe showed serious depression. Her puffy face revealed that she'd cried intensely. She shuffled her feet as she walked toward me. As I watched the vision unfold, the Lord said, "Don't go there."*

I called Anita and told her my vision. We prayed that God would show her the beauty in her life and not let her go down a road of despair. Though I didn't fully understand what I had seen, Holy Spirit did. A couple days later, I knew it meant much more than I had initially thought.

On Sunday, we were on our family Zoom meeting. To check on her dogs, Anita wandered to the back door that led to her patio, the same door where I stood in my vision. She began to scream and opened the door after she saw her precious Shih Tzu Isabella with her nose on a rattlesnake's head. She knew poison from that baby rattler would be deadly if the dog were bitten on the nose, close to the brain. All her sisters on Zoom began to pray loudly, authoritatively, and fervently to call protection over that dog. When Anita cajoled the dogs to come into the house, they all complied. A deputy later arrived to catch that diamondback rattler, and it lay immobile long enough for him to get it into a bucket and carry it out to the desert (see Appendix #12). Then it became active like a normal, baby rattlesnake.

I'm still rejoicing for the many miracles this event demonstrated. Holy Spirit warned in advance by showing the precious dog ornament on the back patio. Not only her cherished Izzy, but each of those dogs was valuable to Him. Anita "happened" to be at the back door at just the right time. Her sisters "happened" to be there to pray and rebuke that danger the enemy had intended. Anita's dogs rarely come in easily; but they "happened" to obey immediately that day, even the ones that aren't primarily house pets. They were all important to Him, and so was Anita. Father also protected our sister physically because she could've been bitten herself if she'd gone farther outside before seeing the snake. He also protected her emotionally. If one of her dogs had been killed, her reaction would have been like I saw in the vision. The Lord loved Anita, the dogs, and even the snake which was relocated alive and well.

Incidentally, Anita has sent a couple videos that showed orbs on her security camera in her foyer. What's mind-boggling is that one shows all her dogs following her down the hall. Behind the dogs, orbs are trailing them. His creations are truly precious to Him. What an amazing God to create His divine "happenstances" to protect what's dear to us and to Him!

His Protection

Other instances of His protection happened while on my higher journey. During this time, a new Covid variant evolved, and people were again infected. Some whom we knew died. Despite my being in a high-risk category, I'd gotten lax about distancing myself from people or wearing my mask. Within just weeks four people who'd been near me tested positive. One was a woman who'd responded to a word of knowledge I'd had at church one Sunday morning. Though I'd worn my mask, I'd been close to her face and clutched her hands as I prayed. When I heard about her positive status, the enemy tried to make me react in fear. I realized Holy Spirit had given me that word for that specific woman. He protects us as we obey His directives. I learned that long ago.

I was an infant when my parents took our family on vacation to Arizona. They felt Holy Spirit leading them to go a few miles into Mexico to do missionary work. However because the area was experiencing a smallpox epidemic, the border was closed. That wasn't a problem for the Lord. My parents had access each time they went, and miracles occurred during those Mexico trips. Encouraged by God's provision and access to people He'd sent them to, they drove back to Ohio praising Father for all they'd seen. Then, I got sick. A library book about smallpox told my mother that symptoms and incubation time paralleled what was going on with me.

Mom, a fairly new Christian, could've let fear for her baby's health override faith, but she had fallen in love with her Savior. She knew He didn't send His warriors on missions and let them be part of satan's casualties. He didn't put front-line workers' families in danger as they traveled the road of obedience. She refused to accept my sickness. I got well. She sometimes testified about it over the years as I grew up, but she didn't make the connection when I started kindergarten and had to get a second smallpox shot because the first one didn't take. That one failed too. When a third shot didn't work as I started college, the doctor declared I had natural immunity.

When I told my mother, she just tilted her head with the quizzical look my family knew well. "Hmm, I thought you had smallpox." That story became a memorial pillar to me, so I applied it all these years later to Covid exposures. By the way, I didn't get sick from any of those times when I was exposed to infected people in services. When He sends you, He covers you, for the "glory [*kabod*] of the Lord shall be your rear guard" (Isa. 58:8). He has been, is, and will be!

Light My Path

During the winter of 2021, wonders occurred which showed me again that Father loves His kids so very much. I've held onto this scripture: "And so we have the prophetic word confirmed, which you do well to heed as a light that shines in a dark place" (2 Pet. 1:19). When I've been unsure how to proceed, I quote this promise for Holy Spirit to light my path, and He does. During my *higher* journey, that word was again real as He showed Himself in simple yet mighty ways.

The Story Is Unfolding

One snowy Saturday morning, Wade and I shoveled sidewalks at the building where we would teach Monday's class. When we started to leave, I couldn't find my keys, so I panicked. That key ring accessed all the doors in my life. Several times I meticulously combed through each pile I'd shoveled. No keys. Because we needed to leave, I prayed that God would protect them until we located them. I also quoted my go-to scripture. What I know, have known, and will know is that the Lord is faithful!

That night before I fell asleep, I again asked Holy Spirit to light my path. I saw a vision of a snow pile Wade had shoveled. The next morning I told him the location I'd seen in the vision. I said I'd probably dropped them from my pocket onto the sidewalk he was scraping. He could've overlooked the keys as they plunged to the bottom of that fluffy snow. After church, I attended my Sunday Zoom meeting with one sister, Lynda, who prayed authoritatively for God to let us find them that day. By the time I signed off the Zoom call and went downstairs, Wade was in the kitchen dangling my keys. They were exactly where the vision had instructed. I rejoiced all week.

A few days later, Holy Spirit again showed His faithfulness to light my path. I'd lain down earlier than usual and realized I hadn't seen Cleo, our calico kitten, since before I'd fed the cats that night. Going more than three hours without her climbing onto my lap to snuggle was unusual. I scoured the house, rattling treats and plates to make her think she was being fed. She didn't come despite multiple attempts. She was a rescue cat that had been born in our neighbor's window well. Eventually, the mama cat brought her to live on our deck. Because she'd begun her life outside, I stuck my head out the front and back doors and called her name. No Cleo. Again I stood on first-hand experience, my scripture, and my knowledge of God's faithfulness. I once more asked Him to light my path. Suddenly, I remembered that when she lived in the backyard, she ran under the deck to hide if anything (lawnmowers, barking dogs, etcetera) scared her.

Bundled in my coat, I proceeded outside to the deck. This time, I *shouted* her name. Immediately, she squealed back. I yelled again, and so did she. As I went down the deck's stairs, there she stood beneath the steps' protection, waiting for me to pick her up rather than have her tender paws trudge through frigid snow to get to me. When I gently lifted Cleo and hugged her against me, she burrowed beneath the warmth of my coat. Lord, You were again faithful. Our God loves us so much that everything about our lives matters to Him. How do you need Him to light your path? A business deal? A person who wants to date you? A house you may buy? Lost keys? A kitten who darted out the back door? Just like God protected my sister's dogs and a rattlesnake, whatever's important to you is more important to Him. HE IS FAITHFUL!

HEALINGS

We experienced wondrous healings and miracles in our services and daily lives during this time of seeking *higher*. One Sunday morning, a friend approached me at the end of service during altar ministry. Her nephew was dying of Covid in an ICU. Another lady and I joined hands and prayed for our friend. A tangible anointing fell as we made Scripture-based declarations. The situation changed. Her nephew survived although doctors said he wouldn't. By week's end he was down to 50 percent on the ventilator and was released later.

During this time the Lord healed often through words of knowledge. For example, one Monday I received a word about kidney stones. Before worship that night, a couple came for prayer time. I told the wife about the word of knowledge and asked for everyone to pray. The lady said her daughter and son-in-law were on vacation, and he was having extreme pain because of kidney stones. We prayed and claimed that word for him. Hundreds of miles away, the discomfort left, and he was pain-free for the rest of their vacation.

One Monday night during worship, a lady received a word of knowledge about something she didn't understand—tardive dyskinesia, a nervous system condition resulting from certain medications. None of us had heard of it nor even knew how to pronounce it. That happens sometimes when God uses us humans with limited knowledge to relay something beyond our ability. Wade asked if anyone knew what that was, and young man blurted out its meaning. He'd been diagnosed with it, and God wanted him to know that He knew and cared about everything concerning him. That was a powerful *higher* event.

One Friday during our Zoom morning worship time, I saw a vision of a puffy eye. I shared that, but the ailment didn't describe any of us. We always teach that sometimes Holy Spirit wants us to put something on the shelf until it comes to fruition. The following Monday, as Wade taught class, I took requests from the Facebook chat. One viewer said someone's grandmother was in emergency surgery after she'd fallen, and something had penetrated her eye. We prayed with authority because of the word of knowledge from a few days before. One of the ladies in class felt led to follow up on that healing. God told her to take a prayer cloth for the granddaughter to put on the eye. She took it to their house; and as they laid the cloth on her eye without vision, they prayed. When they removed the prayer cloth, she could see some objects.

Another Sunday afternoon, I met with two of my sisters on Zoom. A nephew, brother-in-law, and another sister had been diagnosed with Covid. We all felt a foreboding that we needed to seek the Lord seriously for our family. God was in our midst and Anita travailed. All of us in the meeting discovered gold dust on our hands. In the next few days, good reports arrived. The glory that pervades our seeking Him brings many blessings. A powerful presence and victory accompanies our readiness and obedience.

The Fast

Other healings happened in our family. My daughter discovered a lump in her breast. After a mammogram and ultrasound, doctors ordered a biopsy. Because of the mass' shape and size, they told her the growth was likely malignant. Though I've taught her that we trust the Lord in hard situations and despite doctors' reports, she was distressed. At our next Zoom meeting, my sisters and I agreed to fast for my daughter and a nephew who had a growth in his abdomen. We'd begun holding him up in prayer months earlier regarding this issue plus his foster son's adoption, a process which had already taken more than two years.

The day after the fast, I rose early to drive thirty minutes to an appointment. I hadn't traveled a block before I was compelled to sing words of love to my Savior. An intense angelic presence saturated my car. I knew those angels had come for healings. Maneuvering on the crooked, country road, I called out names of my daughter, nephew, and others with healing needs. As various people came to mind, I stretched my hand toward their geographical direction. The angelic presence persisted and reminded me of more people's needs to pray for until I reached my destination.

When I shared this experience with my sisters at our next Zoom meeting, Anita said the same thing had happened to her. Angels showed up at her house the night before my morning angelic trip. They accomplished their purpose. God's glory covered the Southwest and Midwest to accomplish healings and miracles, including a sister who had a bad case of Covid which broke that day. Despite the doctor's fears, my daughter's biopsy revealed a benign mass. Not only did my nephew's adoption finalize; but after those days of fasting and angelic visits, word came back. The abdomen growth had shrunk forty-five percent. A few months later my nephew told his mom he couldn't feel it anymore. At his one-year appointment, doctors said the tumor looked dead and that my nephew's case was one for the record books. It's now dissolved and being expelled from his body. Once again God's love and faithfulness to my family was demonstrated mightily.

However God wasn't finished. That same nephew's eleven-year-old daughter also needed a healing a few months later. After doctors found a knot on her leg, we prayed and fasted for a couple of weeks. Though doctors thought it was likely a cyst, the diagnosis everyone dreads came back from the lab—cancer. We continued to fast and pray for this lovely young girl. About a week and a half later, more extensive pathology revealed it was a benign tumor. What an amazing Lord Who can change doctors' reports!

Another sister had been diagnosed with a cyst on her liver several years earlier. Not only did her sisters and brothers pray and fast for her, but many other prayer warriors kept her on their hearts and in their prayers. A report finally came back and said the cyst had shrunk so much that her doctor said it was essentially gone. He raved about her remarkable, unusual progress. His words were, "That never happens," and he called her the "Poster child for this disease." Of course, my sister gave credit to God. Big things aren't big anymore when we give them to the consummate Healer.

My Brother

In June of the first year of going higher, I taught a class on the glory using the first three chapters of Ezekiel. I shared pictures of signs, wonders, and revelations from my past along with new experiences that had happened since the call to *higher*. Just seeing those pictures strengthened my faith. About a year later, we needed to rely on faith and knowledge that God had performed and would perform awe-inspiring miracles. Another family crisis occurred when my brother Jason fell during a seizure and hit his head. As a result, he had two brain bleeds. Because his wife was out-of-town, he lay without medical help for more than a day. His chance of survival was bleak. However even before he was taken to the hospital, my family and many others went to prayer.

We interceded for him before, during, and after his brain surgery. He made it through the surgery, but his body temperature wasn't recovering as well as doctors hoped. One Thursday night Anita and I met on Zoom, and she felt led to sing "The Blessing." While it played on YouTube, we both felt a great anointing in our homes which were 2,000 miles apart. Oil appeared on my fingers and forehead. As we prayed, I was led to rub the heavenly oil on top of my head for Jason. As an angelic presence engulfed us, I should've sat there and soaked in the manifestation. However I realized I could put the oil-drenched fingers on Wade's forehead too. I told Anita I was going upstairs to cover him. However by the time I got to where he was sleeping, the oil had dried up. The Lord had sent that phenomenon for Jason.

That night, Anita felt led to inform our family that we were going to worship together on Saturday, but I attended a funeral which lasted longer than expected. At the exact time my family was getting together for worship, the praise team at the funeral celebration did their final song— "The Blessing." Nothing is a coincidence with God. That day, my brother's fever broke, though for days they'd unsuccessfully tried every medical measure.

Around this same time, a friend had a word of knowledge. She smelled sulfur and had extreme pain in her arm. That odor is one which exudes from abandoned mines where Anita lives in Arizona and where Jason had grown up. He had also hurt his arm when he fell. This revelation was from a lady who didn't know Jason, but she played a part in his healing process. Within a few days, he was speaking, sitting up, out of ICU, and released to rehab. His arm was fine. Because of his unbelievable progress, when the doctor came to check on him, he took a second look at Jason's chart to confirm he was the same person. Jason was discharged from the hospital and rehab center much earlier than had been anticipated. He went home with a few restrictions, but he didn't even require speech therapy after the head surgery. The Lord loved my little brother so much that Holy Spirit illuminated a path for others to intercede on his behalf. That's *higher*.

VISIONS

Jesus

As some of us worshiped before class one night, the anointing came in strongly. Even sitting at the keyboard was difficult for me. When I stood, I had what I call my Gumby legs—they didn't want to hold me up. As I soaked in that thick presence, I had a vision:

PART FOUR | FROM GLORY TO GLORY

An arched doorway revealed glory so dense and bright that it seemed like fire. Jesus' silhouette appeared and stood as He gazed at us. He came out the arched doorway and put His hands on the heads of those bowing in reverence. As we all kept bowing, He stood near, lingered a while, and continued touching us. On the floor were human ribs opened to display organs, blood, muscles, and tendons. Jesus was barefoot and trod through those ribs. He was tender and took His time.

I knew that what looks like a mess is precious to Him. The touch from His nail-scarred hands or even His feet brings miracles. That *touch* is *haptomai*, "to attach oneself to."[135] When the woman with the issue of blood touched His garment or His healing hand raised Jairus' daughter, both were *haptomai* (see Matt. 9:20, 25). His touch attaches healing from a Carpenter's rough hands. But His feet, tired and dusty from Middle Eastern roads, or His garment's battered hem brings healing too. It grips like Velcro or Super Glue. Whether you touch Jesus or He touches you, He *haptomais* you.

During class that night, we prayed for anyone who had situations to which this vision might refer because ribs cover many of our bodies' organs. I later received an email from one lady who'd been in that worship atmosphere before class. She perceived an additional meaning. Ribs house our hearts. She said the Lord is bringing a "blanket of submission" on America that will fall upon hearts. He'll have access to our hearts as our ribs are laid open. It will be brought about by His touch that produces humility. Lord, let us crave You as we submit to what you want for us.

The Light

Glory and light are often connected. When an angel delivered Peter from prison, a light shone in the jail (see Acts 12:7). While Paul talked to King Agrippa, he described his Damascus Road experience and said he "saw a light from heaven, brighter than the sun, shining around [him] and those who journeyed with [him]" (Acts 26:13). That account is similar to the brightness I've seen accompanying His glory. One night before streaming, I saw a vision about the light:

A person was sitting in a small boat resembling a carnival ride. The raft was entering a cave. From my vantage point, I could peer into that cavern with darkness as far as I could see. The Lord gave me a message to share: "Don't go. Turn back into the light!"

Feeling urgency at the beginning of class, I shared the vision with those attending in person or on Facebook Live. Then we prayed as a group. Before week's end, someone who viewed the class on Facebook approached me. As a recovering addict, she'd been drug-free a long time. However she'd recently endured such intense trials that she was contemplating returning to drugs. She'd tuned in to class and heard the message Holy Spirit had given: "Don't go. Turn back into the light!" She responded, received God's communication, and took it to heart. She circled back to the light, and her mindset changed. She no longer wanted what she'd left behind. What an awesome God Who sees us and cares! He loved that lady so much that He addressed her personally.

His Presence On The Plane

Several months into my higher journey, I flew to visit my daughter. During the flight, I labored to edit book chapters. I soon grew tired of working, so I tried to nap. Because sleep is a rare occurrence for me on a plane, I gave up that hope and began to pray silently. That was what Holy Spirit had wanted me to do all along. Suddenly, an angelic presence pressed against me. With such a strong anointing, the thought occurred to me that maybe angels were there to protect our flight from danger. They actually came for a different, splendid reason.

In that anointing, my discreet prayers were no longer silent but had a quiet-but-definite sound. Worship accompanied them, and multiple revelations to share with friends and family came faster than I could write. In my worship/prayer mode, no one looked at the weird, little woman perched on the aisle in Row Five. An empty middle seat separated me from a hearing-impaired lady by the window. The engine's loud growl below and various conversations from mandatory-masked faces muffled my sounds, so they were indistinct enough to keep from annoying others. During my time from Indianapolis to Oklahoma City, God communicated much.

Something which still thrills me is that Holy Spirit revealed a need for a flight attendant and made it possible for me to pray for him. When I saw a vision of something across his forehead, I knew he needed prayer. However, communicating with that busy attendant was difficult, so I prayed silently. The third time I saw the vision, I asked God to give me an opportunity. He did, about a minute later. The young man walked back the aisle and met another attendant right by my seat. I didn't delay in acting on the God-ordained opportunity, so I tapped his arm. After he bent over, I explained that I was a Christian minister, and I felt led to pray for his forehead. His response wasn't negative as I had anticipated. He placed his hand on my arm as a sign of acceptance. When I finished praying, he laid his head on top of mine to acknowledge what I had said and done.

For the remainder of the flight, I stayed in awe not only about the revelation but about his reaction. As we were deplaning, he stood in the front of the cabin and watched me inch down the aisle. When I passed by, I thanked him for letting me pray.

He hugged me. "No!" he said. "Thank you!"

As with many revelations, I may never know how God touched that young man's life, but I'm certain He did. The glory shows up for a purpose. Though we don't see results, we can be sure something has been accomplished.

EXTREME GLORY

Arches

During my journey I've had many visions about God's extreme glory. For example, Wade began noon-time prayer on Facebook. The first day, I worshiped beforehand and saw this vision:

> *An arched entrance stood with a brick wall blocking it. The top and sides of the wall left too little space for anyone to squeeze through, but I had a limited view beyond it. Magnificent structures, tall with unique architecture, lined the streets. Domed roofs were gold and had lights with a golden hue. I knew I was looking at His extreme glory. I needed to knock down the wall so I could get through to experience it, not just view it.*

That glory outshone anything I've seen. The light was white and bright with a translucent, yet shiny hue. I thought of John's description of how New Jerusalem will have no sun nor moon, for God's glory shines so brightly (see Rev. 21:23). The next day in prayer time, I again worshiped, and a weighty *kabod* again entered. For a second time, I saw the vision of the glory and arch:

> *The arch still had the brick obstruction in front of the entrance, but this time I didn't see buildings beyond it. Instead an extremely thick cloud of bright yellow and gold partially covered the wall where the*

> *gaps had been. I knew the wall wouldn't need to be broken down by human hands. The glory would cover it and allow entrance.*

Bricks are man's efforts both to create and to use for building. God's glory doesn't involve our work, but rather positioning ourselves so we can access His consuming presence which creates, builds, or tears down. When Ezekiel saw the temple filled with arches, he was told that priests couldn't wear anything which caused sweat (see 44:18). Going into His glory doesn't depend on our efforts. We can enter as we allow worship to usher us in.

A few months later, I again saw the bright glory in another vision:

> *At first I viewed a silver, camel-back chest with ornate designs. When it opened, an overwhelmingly bright, golden light shone from inside the chest. I saw God's massive treasure of which I could partake. However, though the lock was open, I had to detach another piece of the lock before I could access the treasure of His extreme glory. Once before, I'd seen a vision of a lock with the top part broken off but still in the latch. This prevented the door from opening to allow entrance. In that vision and this one with the arched chest, His all-consuming, extreme glory was there for the asking, but I needed to remove another obstacle that impeded my entering fully.*

I know He was telling me I had to do something else before I could enter into that place of extreme glory. I need Him to reveal what will open the door to *higher*. Twice, He has told me I needed to open it. I know breakthrough will come through worship, but I'm waiting for Him to reveal what I need to do and how I need to do it.

Strength

My visions about arches made me curious. Arches have a place in history. Roman engineers built roads with arches. They were also used in Egyptian pyramid architecture. The oldest existing one is in Thebes and is dated around 1350 B.C. However existing remains of an arch connect Zion and Moriah.[136] Symbolically an arch has many meanings. Because it's a geometrical shape which carries great strength, the archway I saw likely symbolized support and strength. Triumphal arches were erected to commemorate a grand event. The arch in my visions framed a doorway to a higher glory walk. Being in the glory is truly grand.

The only biblical references to arches are by Ezekiel, who spoke of them several times. His archways often were part of a grouping of beveled windows, gateways, and palm trees. In Chapter 40 when God revealed to Ezekiel the new city and temple, arches were *elammah*, "a pillar-space (or colonnade), i.e. a pale (or portico)."[137] That word is likely derived from *ayil*, meaning "strength . . . anything strong . . . a pilaster . . . strong support); an oak or other strong tree: . . . mighty."[138] One reference included archways, palm trees, and seven *steps* (see 40:22), the same word as when Amos described *layers* to Heaven (see Amos 9:6). As I said earlier, the number seven has many meanings including man's spiritual perfection. Later Ezekiel would see eight steps (see 40:31). Eight is a number indicating new beginnings. To me, those numbers signify that when we climb higher, we reach a realm of spiritual perfection which takes us into a new beginning in God.

When I saw the arches vision, I knew I was in His extreme glory and would experience it more. In one vision that year:

> *I saw an emblem near the top of a stem that extended high but was also planted in soil. At the top was something fluffy like a feather or puffy branch. The entire picture seemed to be a crest denoting rank like on a shield.*

Layers

Several weeks later, the anointing came in powerfully during home worship. I had another vision which made this first one clearer:

> *I again saw a long stem. Something like a plume stretched high on top. Instead of a feather, it was bright lights flaring like fireworks. The bottom was again planted in dirt. A cross-section of the ground showed layers like at the Grand Canyon where a variety of levels reflect different eras. Where the pointed part went into dirt, crude oil spewed.*

As I watched this vision unfold, I realized Holy Spirit was revealing another *higher* message. Father communicated several times with me using layers and stairs during this journey. These levels illustrate various depths and heights we can attain in the glory. The top part that I'd seen twice carried the most powerful glory into the highest tier. The rank it denoted was extreme, and that glory could accomplish anything. Through the extreme glory, we have access to many benefits including healing and provision (crude oil), two of *Jehovah*'s redemptive names—*Rapha* and *Jireh*. I realized crude oil could also refer to Holy Spirit, and much more was available from Him as we persevere into that extreme level.

I continued to watch the great glory explosion for a while and grew distracted:

> *As my attention waned, the glory pole grew shorter and not as remarkable. The rod was still connected to the earth, but the layers were lower.*

We humans, dust of the earth, can reside in any layer and still experience God's glory to varying degrees; but to witness astonishing signs, wonders, and miraculous events, we must be in that high, extreme level. When we choose *higher*, "Eye has not seen, nor ear heard, nor have entered into the heart of man the things which God has prepared for those who love Him" (1 Cor. 2:9). We can't fathom what can happen. That night as the vision in the extreme glory unfolded, I called for healings, especially dizziness Wade had been experiencing. For more than a year, he'd unsuccessfully gone through several tests to determine the cause. I prayed for him in that presence but didn't tell him about that prayer. The next day, I noticed he didn't grab onto furniture and countertops to prevent a fall. In the highest glory layer, Wade's balance had been healed.

More

As with other aspects of this journey, those layers reminded me of various levels in the river in Ezekiel's vision (see Ezek. 47). The deeper he went, the more signs and wonders occurred. Because He "is able to do exceedingly abundantly above all that we ask or think, according to the power that works in us" (Eph. 3:20), that power which works in and through us produces greater miracles as we climb higher. In addition to Wade's healing, I knew as I watched the extreme glory vision that more than healing and provision were available in the extreme glory. This was the *higher* message again where unlimited, unbelievable miracles were not just possible, but probable. I saw more fireworks in a vision a day later:

> *In His presence, a deep-red, thick consistency framed the sky. I knew this represented cancer because I'd seen it in a vision years before. At the bottom of the picture, I saw the fireworks of extreme glory. I watched as the extreme glory ate up cancer like Pac-Man.*

While still in that glory, Holy Spirit gave direction and a prophetic action. The next day was Sunday; as a church body, we needed to enter God's extreme glory. During worship we should stand by the altar in faith to eradicate cancer in those who personally suffered with it and those for whom we could stand in proxy. I texted Stacey, our worship leader, and said what I felt led to do. She immediately agreed. Holy Spirit had been speaking to her saying that the next morning's worship needed to accomplish something, but she wasn't sure what that would be until I contacted her. In the worship service the next day, extreme glory pervaded our presence. The anointing was so powerful that many, including me, couldn't stand and were slain in the Spirit at the altar.

I again saw extreme glory like sparklers or fireworks one night during worship before class:

> *I saw a lock that a skeleton key would fit into. In the opening of the lock, an angel stood with his head in the top round part and his robe flaring out at the bottom. Leading up to him, a line was on fire like a sparkler. It reminded me of how a streak of fire would start in the distance away from an explosive then burn until it reached the dynamite. I knew when it got to the angel, a mighty reaction would occur, and the door would open to extreme glory.*

I was reminded of Ezekiel's first glory visions. He depicted living creatures like burning coals of fire and torches going back and forth. He described the fire as bright with flashes of lightning going forth from it (see 1:13–14). God's glory is powerful and intense, similar to fireworks, lightning, sparklers, and dynamite. He's described as using lightning: "He covers His hands with lightning, and commands it to strike" (Job 36:32). As we worshiped, we witnessed His mighty, lightning presence.

Climbing Higher

Layers I'd seen showed levels of glory and had the same message God gave me previously in the stairs' dream and visions. Layers are mentioned in an Amos scripture I previously referenced. In a description of God, he says, "He who builds His layers in the sky, and has founded His strata in the earth . . . —the Lord is His name" (Amos 9:6). The word *layers* is *ma'alah* meaning "elevation . . . journey to a higher place . . . climactic progression . . . things that come up . . . stair . . . ."[139] *Ma'alah* is often preceded by the word *shîr* or *shîrâ* meaning *song*.[140] Together they speak of ascending stairs to a higher level. Those layers in my vision correspond to stairs where an unimaginable level of extreme glory exists.

The concept of climbing higher is demonstrated by the ascent to the temple of the Lord. For yearly festivals, Hebrews would sing a *shîrâ* during their journey up the hill into Jerusalem and on the steps leading to the temple.[141] Psalms Chapters 120–134 are known as the Ascents, which were likely sung by priests as they climbed the temple steps.[142] Written during exile, these Psalms speak of their oppression and a longing to go home, having peace and resurgence of a strong Jerusalem, and awaiting the Messiah.[143] Again, these scriptures relate to worship's part in the *higher* journey. This ascent excursion is accompanied by worship. We also must ascend to new levels of worship to get to higher levels of glory.

Habakkuk said, "The earth will be filled with the knowledge of the glory of the Lord, as the waters cover the sea" (Hab. 2:14). The word for *filled* is *male'*, "to fill or . . . be full of . . . fulfil."[144] It means "fulfilling one's word . . . to declare that one will do something and then to do it." It's the Old Testament word which describes being filled with Holy Spirit.[145] Not only the Habakkuk scripture but also Jeremiah quotes God as saying He fills the heaven and earth (see Jer. 23:24). Jesus declared Holy Spirit would come, and it was fulfilled. What an amazing advantage that His gift to us, Holy Spirit, now lives inside us and takes us to higher glory levels! As we ascend through worship, we become more and more filled with the knowledge of the Lord.

PROPHETIC WORDS

The Valley

As I've been seeking the glory, Holy Spirit has given many revelations. One day after worship, I saw this vision:

> *A white circle was made of something like acrylic. Inside was a second silver, shiny circle surrounding another solid-white circle. That was a button to push. God's finger appeared and authoritatively pressed it. That button's purpose was to initiate a launch.*

I believe Holy Spirit was saying a glory event is getting ready to propel us higher, and His finger will bring it on. I later had another vision:

PART FOUR | FROM GLORY TO GLORY

> *I saw God but not His face. He stood over the Midwest. Behind Him were lines that intersected to form a large X. I knew X marked the spot. I wondered if Wade and I would go out from our location in the Midwest to various places to minister or if that would be a target for the enemy. Months later, I saw something that resembled an apple slicer. A circle in the middle had several lines going out in different directions.*

At first I thought this was describing what our expanded ministry would be. Wade has felt for years that we would operate an apostolic hub where we'd train others by teaching about Holy Spirit's gifts. Perhaps this is confirming that Wade's prophecy is imminent. However I wondered a few months later if these visions could have prophesied about a renewal revival, even the reference to the Midwest. God's finger started in Kentucky at the Asbury Outpouring and spread to other places like an apple slicer. Silver means atonement while white is purity and righteousness. Like Holy Spirit had shown in a previous vision, a circle is never-ending and worldwide. I believe these relate to God's end-time army He's raising up.

End-Time Army

In the temple God told the man (angel) instructing Ezekiel to put a mark on the foreheads of men who grieved about the nation's sins (see 9:4). The word for *mark* is *taw*, the last letter of the Hebrew alphabet. It resembles an X or cross. Like the blood above the door in Egypt (see Exod. 12:13), that mark meant those people would be protected. God would safeguard the righteous remnant which was to arise.[146] His remnant will be important in the end-time army.

Throughout my journey the Lord showed me a recurring revelation about the end-time army. One night, intense anointing during worship pervaded our house. After finishing, I sat, soaked, and purposely didn't let my mind wander which happened too frequently. Then I saw an evolving vision:

> *I was at the top of a mountain. I'm not sure whether I was on it or hovering above. Different mountain ranges created a circular pattern. Those mountains surrounded a round valley or chasm far below. Trees were thick and lush, and I thought that if anyone had to go through that valley, he or she would have difficulty because of the dense foliage. I wondered if I would cross it. As I stared at the chasm,*

The Story Is Unfolding

> *several army-like vehicles in the distance plowed through the middle, mowing down trees as they progressed. That created an enormous road. The scene reminded me of the Red Sea's parting. I watched without fear but rather curiosity. I saw a door with a bronze plaque above it that mentioned a city in Canada.*

Though I'm still not sure of the significance of Canada, I got messages from this vision. At the same time I was seeing this, Holy Spirit spoke to Wade—new levels of power. Mountains often mean revelation while trees can represent people. This vision indicated that an end-time army will arise with new levels of power, and Holy Spirit will cut a path through the thick growth that's hindering progress. Again, a never-ending circle is worldwide. It will be a miraculous act of Holy Spirit to create a new "road in the wilderness" (see Isa. 43:19). Perhaps the hub will be in Canada.

The Ranks

In early autumn of the first year of my *higher* quest, I had seen a vision about the army:

> *A few warriors in full armor sat on white horses in the distance. Their helmets had plumes. They were looking around, and I initially thought they had no direction. I realized they were waiting for others to join their ranks. As I watched, riders went to where the first ones sat. Some farther out started my way. For a moment, I lost the vision. Then I saw it again. Horses and riders were no longer distant but were assembled in a circle; I was part of that group. Those who'd been far away weren't close to me yet, but others had drawn beside me. One warrior was so near, I could have touched him if I reached out.*

This vision reminds me of when John saw Jesus coming on a white horse. A few verses later, armies of Heaven were also on white horses (see Rev. 19:11, 14). I think this vision again refers to the believers' end-time army. This was another message about the remnant coming together. After we had astounding anointing in the extreme glory at church that morning, the next week during worship, many of us again went to the altar. Although this time the anointing wasn't as intense, I saw another vision:

> *A soldier wore a helmet without a brush or feather like ones I'd seen before. Instead, a spike adorned the top. He wasn't in the distance but stood so close I could clearly see and even touch his face.*

This helmet spike was called a Pickelhaube. It was pointed on top and worn mostly in the Nineteenth and Twentieth Centuries by German or Prussian officers. Made of hardened leather, it not only symbolized aggressiveness but also was used to repel swords aimed at the head. This reminded me of when God told Ezekiel not to let others' reactions invade his emotions. God was protecting his thinking just as He does ours. During trench warfare in World War I, materials to make Pickelhaubes were scarce, and the spike often made the wearer more easily spotted by the enemy. As a result, these helmet adornments were later eliminated and replaced by something more practical and effective.[147] The Pickelhaube was from older days, but it had served its purpose. We can't become stuck in what God did in the past but must realize He has something new for us, even in the weapons He chooses.

A few months later, I saw this same vision:

> *Now, the circle was closer together. Officers rode down the middle heading my way while awaiting the impending battle. I knew they were closing ranks.*

"Closing ranks" refers to when a group has harmony; and "they make an effort to stay united, especially in order to defend themselves from severe criticism.[148] That definition was a warning to me. Like when God cautioned Ezekiel that criticism could derail his assignment, we Christians must know disapproval will come even from within God's army. We should expect it and close ranks against the enemy instead of fighting each other. We must draw the remnant together in order for the church to arise.

Later, in a similar vision:

> *I was walking along an unpaved road or path. I wasn't in a hurry and didn't recognize the location, but the terrain resembled a prairie state. I continued walking and saw my destination. At the bottom of a slight hill was a rounded area made up of the same dirt road. About five or six other streets or paths led to that zone. As I got nearer, I saw people converging onto the circular area at the end of each path. Though we came from different directions and took dissimilar paths, we'd each arrive at the bottom circle.*

Again, this message was about God's army closing ranks. Our position in that army may not be as leaders riding horses or commanding troops. We may be stationed in less-desirable or various locations—in prairies and coming from different directions. Whatever job the Lord has given in His end-time army, we should close ranks and work for the Kingdom. This vision had similar components with other visions. We were converging on a circle that came together in the middle like an apple slicer.

God's Judgment

In another vision, God was getting ready to bring judgment:

> *He was in the sky, positioned in the Northeastern United States. As He blew on the dust of the earth, it swirled up in a cloud of black.*

Perhaps He was saying He'll stir things up in this country beginning in the Northeast. I also wondered if perhaps these geographical directions could represent Russia (north) and China (east).

> *In a later vision, I saw Him unzipping the earth to release something. Several months later during morning devotions, I heard these things: "A great army shall arise from the east. A great storm will come. Mountains shall tumble."*

Later in the year, I saw two visions:

> *First, a sunset was in the West. Its rays were beneath the horizon, but the sun itself wasn't. A great bracket cradled the sun so it couldn't go down. God was waiting, delaying judgment a little longer to allow those who hadn't yet accepted Him to come or those who'd wandered off to return. In the second vision, I saw a huge pagan plaque with a picture of a god in the middle. Though merely an object, the god on the plaque seemed to come alive. Pale and frightened, he knew his time was limited.*

God may delay His judgment, but judgment will happen. Noah's building of the *ark* took 120 long years. During that time God gave others opportunities for repentance, but they didn't repent (see Gen. 6:13–17). Though Noah, like Ezekiel, could've faced discouragement that made him stop following God's directives, he still proceeded despite others' dismissive reception of the message. We must have perseverance to do our jobs in this end-time army. The sun is ready to set on this world. This vision is saying that God loves His creations so much He wants to give yet another chance.

Later, I saw two more similar visions:

> *In the first, a great tornado hovered above a certain location on earth, though I'm not sure where. In the second, missiles were lined*

> *in a row, slanted and aimed at a particular target. Again, like my earlier vision of the sun, the rockets were waiting. I later wondered if this was the foretelling of the war between Palestine and Israel.*

Several months later, I saw another vision that repeated many things God had said:

> *A whirlwind was coming my way. Its swirling cloud wasn't approaching vertically but horizontally. Churning and strengthening, it drew closer. I saw in its swirls, items that had been swept up inside. I didn't see people but animals and other unidentifiable objects.*

I thought of Ezekiel's experience when he saw a great whirlwind coming from the north. It was a huge cloud of great fire, burning anything around and then engulfing and devouring itself. From the brightness emerged living creatures (see Ezek. 1:4–5). Whirlwinds represent the coming of God.[149] They appear for significant events like when Elijah left Elisha's sight in a glory event—a burning chariot of fire and a whirlwind (see 2 Ki. 2:11). This horizontal whirlwind was showing me about power but also our need to be positioned correctly in God. That horizontal positioning of the whirlwind means something else.

I've already talked about the positions in peace offerings that were horizontal (wave) or vertical (heave). Some also say the cross contains symbolism in its vertical and horizontal components. The vertical beam is positioned in the ground (symbol of man). It reaches toward the heavens thus representing our justification by Jesus. It supports the horizontal beam, which represents our constant journey to sanctification and God's help during this journey.[150] Objects being swept away were idols or behaviors Christians hold onto. I knew that intense glory was growing nearer. My husband says it's not *when* the glory move will come but *where*. I want the Lord to select us, and I will go wherever He chooses.

Light and Darkness

After I saw those visions, I later viewed something I'd seen before which related to God's judgment: A thick, dark, threatening cloud likely representing the power of darkness on this earth. Sin's blackness sometimes appears so overwhelming that we Christians can't imagine the depth of human depravity. We should, "Arise, shine; for your light has come! And the glory of the Lord is risen upon you" (Isa. 60:1). Despite what's around us, we must shine in the darkness. Like when Ezekiel spoke to Israel about personal responsibility, each Christian, individually and as a body, should be part of the light that shines in the darkness. Paul says God has commanded light in the darkness. We obey that instruction by first shining light in our hearts so we can show God's glory through Jesus in us (see 2 Cor. 4:6).

Another day I saw a vision which also spoke of light and darkness:

> *Bright light gushed through a large hole in the middle of a dark cloud. The light was gold with a beam traveling down and again pointing to a specific place. I still didn't know where it was. In the beam was a golden crown with a band of gold on the bottom. Above the band was gold webbing that reminded me of a badminton birdie's web.*

Gold means glory. Gold webbing ties us together in one accord. The crown describes our kingship in earth. We have dominion and should be a light to cut a hole in the vast darkness.

I saw a similar vision months later:

> *I watched an area of utter darkness for a short time. On the horizon I saw a sliver of bright light begin horizontally. It grew bigger but not huge. Suddenly a winged horse came from that piece of light.*

The Bible includes descriptions of horses that fly. Elijah was taken by a chariot and horses of fire into the heavens (see 2 Ki. 2:11). John saw the heavens open to show Jesus sitting on a white horse, and "Armies in heaven ... followed Him on white horses" (Rev. 19:14). Again I felt Holy Spirit was showing me that Heaven's armies will be joined by our end-time army.

Dry Bones

Like the message to me about closing ranks, Ezekiel also spoke of hope about coming together. His dry bones revelation began with a glory event—another translation. Ezekiel was set down by the Spirit in a valley full of very dry bones (see 37:1-2). Does that describe today? The list of deceptions satan has thrust upon this generation is long and sad. Even the Christian world is full of dry bones. God said that people in Ezekiel's time thought their "bones [were] dry, [their] hope [was] lost, and [they were] cut off!" He promised He would "open your graves and cause you to come up from your graves, and bring you into the land of Israel" (37:11-12). Though many Christians today have lost hope, God's vow to Ezekiel still applies.

After the Lord deposited him on the ground, He asked Ezekiel, "Can these bones live?" (37:3). God told him to prophesy to bring breath into them. God's new move will bring life back into dry bones and will be proceeded by prophetic words. Most churches shun the gifts; some even teach *against* Holy Spirit. In Ezekiel's vision, the prophetic initiated the miracle of the dry bones coming together. Prophecy often comes to pass in phases. Holy Spirit will use the prophetic and even what seems dead and buried to speak breath and breakthrough for victory.

Ezekiel obeyed God's command; but before the bones came back to life, he heard a noise—a rattling of bones. Sometimes we become discouraged when the only response to the Lord's proclamations spoken through us is a noise. However that clamor is the precursor for God's "exceedingly great army" to arise (see 37:10). We're now hearing that noise before seeing parts of the body unite, but the rattling comes first. What's making a noise in the Kingdom today?

The noise preceded the bones joining each other piece-by-piece—sinews, flesh, skin. However breath didn't come into the body until God again told Ezekiel to speak to it: "Come from the four winds, O breath, and breathe on these slain that they may live" (see 37:9). Then breath came, and the bones became a great army. Viewing those dry bones could've brought despair to Ezekiel. He might have thought his assignment was too hard, especially when he had to speak tough words. However obedience to God's directives will make that impossibility become reality. What's He telling you to do in His army? It's time to speak life into dry bones so the army arises.

MY HUSBAND'S THOUGHTS

The Pioneer Anointing

Isa. 43:18–19—*"Do not remember the former things, nor consider the things of old. Behold, I will do a new thing, now it shall spring forth: shall you not know it? I will even make a road in the wilderness and rivers in the desert."*

For twenty-seven years, I've written a prophetic word in our newsletter for the coming year. Holy Spirit has impressed me about a mighty release of a "Pioneer Anointing." Webster's Dictionary defines a pioneer as "one of the first of a kind; a characteristic of settlers in new territory; and those who prepare or open a way for others to travel."[151] This divine enablement is to break through and develop new spiritual territory, prepare paths for others' advancement, and settle into a new Holy Spirit dimension of life. Pioneers are Glory-Bearers of God's presence—containers of God, who lives in them! Pioneers aren't satisfied with status quo—what the world calls normal, safe, rational, and proper. They live by prophetic revelation with a burning desire for all life has to offer to build a future for their families and others. The following are characteristics of Pioneers:

Pioneers Seldom Realize What They Accomplish:

Gal. 1:10—*"For do I now persuade men, or God? Or do I seek to please men? For if I still pleased men, I would not be a bond-servant of Christ."*

Pioneers are mission-oriented, focused, and Spirit-driven, dedicated to Kingdom expansion and spiritual elevation for every believer. They're visionaries, as well as practical planners, implementing God's plan for taking new spiritual territory, entering, and settling in the Glory Zone of God's presence. A pioneer's vision is multi-generational. They're foundation builders and seed planters, knowing seeds' power to produce a harvest of souls. Pioneers desire their spiritual ceiling to be the floor for future generations. This is contrary to present-day denominational monuments to past moves of God where men discovered a revelation and formed doctrines around that revelation. They created a museum of what God did, not acknowledging that God's word is vast with greater revelation to discover. The depth of truth as revealed by Holy Spirit is deep; we're barely scratching the surface of what God has made available in Holy Spirit! This is reality of a spiritual pioneer—to explore and settle into a new realm of revelation contained in Scripture and make that revelation become experience in Christ.

Pioneers Seldom Cut a Straight Path:

Heb. 11:8–10—*"By faith Abraham obeyed when he was called to go out to the place which he would receive as an inheritance. And he went out, not knowing where he was going. By faith he dwelt in the land of promise as in a foreign country, dwelling in tents with Isaac and Jacob, the heirs with him of the same promise: for he waited for the city which has foundations, whose builder and maker is God."*

As Abraham envisioned a "city which has foundations, whose builder and maker is God" (Heb. 1:10); so also, pioneers are obsessed with his/her

Spirit-inspired vision. That vision is the blueprint for the future and target for faith to secure its manifestation (see Heb. 11:3). Obstacles, barriers, conflicts, disasters, and enemy arrows don't distract pioneers from pursuing the vision—God's promise, His *rhema* word for him/her. This laser-like focus on God's plan is key to making the vision become inevitable reality by not growing weary in pursuit of destiny (see Gal. 6:9).

Just as Abraham, a pioneer never sets out on a journey without a first-hand, God-given word. When meditated upon, it becomes a vision, then a plan for advancement. Pioneers aren't moved by presumption but by experience in truth through Holy Spirit. Once starting, a pioneer knows detours, roadblocks, and barriers will be a reality and relies upon Holy Spirit for instantaneous guidance and assurance of changes in direction. Pioneers trust God to lead, guide, protect, and provide (see Prov. 3:5-6).

Pioneers Move Forward, Not Backward:

Phil. 3:13-14—*"Brethren, I do not count myself to have apprehended: but one thing I do, forgetting those things which are behind and reaching forward to those things which are ahead, I press toward the goal for the prize of the upward call of God in Christ Jesus."*

Pioneers are accustomed to work, particularly Holy Spirit's motion and momentum to overcome resistance from the realm of darkness. The thief attempts to steal the vision; kill the dream with temporary hardships and obstacles; and destroy God's plan for Kingdom expansion into new, spiritual territory. A God-given vision is always accompanied by a supernatural supply necessary to see it through to manifestation. Too many believers begin a journey to new spiritual territory but turn back when the going becomes tough. They return to familiar, predictable, dead religious ritual. When God gives a vision, He doesn't ask you to do what's practical, plausible, or possible in your ability; His vision is always bigger than your ability! Vision requires Holy Spirit's participation to bring it to fruition. Pioneers understand hardships are stepping-stones to maturity and victory in every situation (see Rom. 5:3; 8:37).

Pioneers Inspire Others:

Acts 4:13—*"Now when they saw the boldness of Peter and John, and perceived that they were uneducated and untrained men, they marveled. And they realized that they had been with Jesus."*

Pioneers are empowered by Holy Spirit to do the same and greater works Jesus promised (see Jn. 14:12). They've been baptized in Holy Spirit and have Jesus' ability to think, speak, and act in Holy Spirit's power (see 1 Cor. 12:4-11). Pioneers have discovered their unique, God-authored gifting(s) and how those gifts work and fit within the church (see 1 Cor. 12:4-11; Eph. 4:11). They understand that Lone Rangers exist only on television, not in the church and that every believer is uniquely gifted to function with others to create a healthy, effective body. Pioneers understand how to inspire, encourage, and motivate by casting a vision big enough for each body member to fit his or her individual gifts and callings within the church's overall mission. They understand that all gifts are necessary to overcome inevitable adversities which will attempt to stop pioneers from moving into God-given destinies (see Jn. 16:33).

Pioneers Embrace Challenges, Not Comfort and Security:

Rom. 15:20-21—*"And so I made it my aim to preach the gospel, not where Christ was named, lest I should build upon another man's foundation, but it is written: 'To whom He was not announced, they shall see: and those who have not heard shall understand.'"*

For pioneers, obstacles, barriers, trials, and tribulations are looked upon as opportunities for Holy Spirit to demonstrate His power and love by overcoming and destroying the devil's works (see 1 Jn. 3:8; Rom. 5:3). Pioneers realize Holy Spirit's gifts operate in situations that need the gifts. Pioneers follow Holy Spirit's leading and are instant to obey the Lord's voice, not caring about others' opinions! They know that when God is with you, nothing can stand against you.

Not all are called to be pioneers. In fact, very few desire to go deeper into the Glory Realm of Holy Spirit. They prefer the safety and security of past revelation—not wanting to be challenged or expand their knowledge and experience in God. But some reading this have felt a stirring in their spirits and breathed a silent *Amen* to this prophetic announcement. To you, I say receive and activate this pioneer anointing and God's vision for your destiny. Meditate on it until God's plan is sure; then step out like Abraham, the original pioneer, to secure your promise!

Epilogue

During my *higher* journey, several people approached me about the church we'd grown up in and which my dad had pastored for about a decade. It was now a neglected building, and people were bemoaning the state of where we'd learned about higher things of God. Truthfully, over the years the building wasn't the only ignored aspect. Various pastors had abandoned something more crucial—operation of Holy Spirit's gifts. People who attended that church as children or young adults were craving those types of services. However during this journey, I again understood that getting deeper or higher in the Lord isn't about a building or a certain ministry. It's individuals desiring and pressing in. It's making a place for the Spirit to move and for others to use their gifts while growing in the process. It's hungering for His move so much that we seek it constantly.

One early morning, I was soaking in His presence and saw another vision:

> A full and beautiful tulip was blooming. Its flowers were dark lavender; each petal's edge sported the same purple, but paler. Time passed, and the flower's fullness dwindled. Eventually, petals fell off and floated to the ground. Behind the tulip's bare stem, I noticed an opening. It appeared to be a dark cave, but I realized the gap was a doorway. An elaborate, wrought-iron frame encircled it. At one time it had been ornate and beautiful; now it was rusty with cobwebs and dust layers. I didn't see a door, just the doorway. Inside, like the wrought-iron frame, deep darkness loomed due to neglect. Wade or I took a broom and dustpan and swept up a dirt pile. In a later vision, I saw two vacuums side-by-side. They were the heavy kind we used when I was a child.

Like my childhood church, this vision refers to a ministry or a church that's fallen into disrepair, spiritually or naturally. Jesus is the Door (see Jn. 10:7); but part of why He came, Holy Spirit, has been largely ignored. Purple often means royalty, power, and kingship, but many don't understand our authority and power. For Wade and me, God was saying that after petals fall off tulips, He'll bring a new season and expanded ministry. Our job will be to bring order and light to what's been neglected or deserted. Concepts I learned in childhood will be crucial for our new assignment. We don't know when or where; but during my journey, we moved to another state about the time tulips were beginning to fade. We're still awaiting fulfillment of our next season. That appointment will be yet another step in the quest for *higher*.

Once, when I became impatient for God's direction, my sister Becky saw a vision of a scroll. It had writing on it, but only about one third was unrolled. She felt Holy Spirit was saying that what has been planned is already written out and will come to pass at the appointed time. We're awaiting pieces to fall together as God wills. He has a purpose and perfect timing for when His assignment comes. But as we wait, the journey is glorious. Lord, You know which doors to open and which to close.

I once asked Wade what *higher* looks like. During this more-than-three-year journey, the Lord has illustrated that often—angelic visits, miracles, a phone ringing in our hallway, and more. I'm still experiencing examples of *higher*, so I wonder when I should finish this book. However I realize my aspirations for *higher* will never be finished. I'll keep recording events in preparation for another volume about higher examples of glory events in the future. A few days ago, I'd again worshiped into the glory. As I sat in His presence, I saw a dripping faucet like those outside of houses. A couple days later, I saw a fountain spurting upward without much intensity. I thought about my dream and the gushing of a tsunami, which led me on this journey. Holy Spirit is again telling me that though I've seen many things so far, this is just the beginning. A drip. A spurt. Much more will come. To be continued . . . .

Endnotes

1. What Is Meaning, *Christianity.com*.
2. "What Is Meaning."
3. "What Is Meaning."
4. Jamieson, *Commentary*, 204.
5. Hayford, *New Spirit Filled Bible*, 114.
6. Hayford, 1094.
7. *Interpreting Dictionary, Holy Bible*, 3.
8. *Interpreting*, 4.
9. Pfeiffer, *Wycliffe Commentary*, 707.
10. Cook, ed., *Barnes Notes*, 299.
11. Feinberg, *Prophecy of Ezekiel*, 17.
12. Hayford, 1094.
13. Feinberg, 11.
14. Dake, *Annotated Reference Bible*, 1364.
15. *Foundation Study Bible*, Nelson, 898.
16. Hayford, 1094.
17. Barnes, 308.
18. Crandall, "Hand of the Lord," *Faithlife.com*/sermons.
19. Jamieson, 203.
20. Hayford, 1094.
21. Wycliffe, 710.
22. Jamieson, 204.
23. Wycliffe, 710.
24. Hayford, 1094.
25. Strong, *Exhaustive Concordance*, H3374.
26. Jamieson, 207.
27. Hayford, 1094.
28. Feinberg, 19.
29. Wycliffe, 710.
30. Barnes 310.
31. Wycliffe, 710.
32. Hayford, 1094.
33. Hayford, 438.
34. Strong, H5375.
35. "Meaning of Colors," colorsexplained.com.

36. Strong, H6963.
37. Hayford, 1095.
38. Feinberg, 25.
39. Feinberg, 20.
40. Jamieson, 207.
41. Barnes, 311.
42. Strong, H3519.
43. Hayford, 1097.
44. *Foundation*, 1088.
45. Cooper, "Seraphim, Cherubim," whyangels.com.
46. Cooper.
47. Cooper.
48. Gordon, "What Is the Ark," livescience.com.
49. Cooper.
50. Jamieson, 205.
51. Cooper.
52. Feinberg, 22.
53. Jamieson, 208.
54. Hayford, 1092.
55. Strong, H8085.
56. Feinberg, 23.
57. Jamieson, 209.
58. Wycliffe, 711.
59. Strong, G2822.
60. Strong, G1588.
61. Hayford, 1395.
62. Strong G1391.
63. Strong, G2999.
64. Feinberg, 12.
65. Hayford, 1142.
66. Dake, 1366.
67. Strong, H7015.
68. Barnes, 312.
69. Jamieson, 209.
70. Hayford, 1096.
71. Hayford, 1096.
72. Feinberg, 27.
73. Barnes, 307.
74. Feinberg, 12.
75. Feinberg, 29.
76. Feinberg, 12.
77. Wycliffe, 711.
78. Strong, H8068.
79. Barnes, 312.
80. Strong, H8068.
81. Dake, 1439.
82. "Interpreting," 4.
83. Feinberg, 25.

Endnotes

84. Feinberg, 30.
85. Strong, G2279.
86. "Ezekiel's Calling," ucg.org.
87. Strong, H7494.
88. Strong, H5401.
89. Strong, H2534.
90. Hayford, 1096.
91. Feinberg, 24.
92. Strong, H8074.
93. Hayford, 1096.
94. Strong, H1697.
95. Jamieson, 211.
96. Feinberg, 29.
97. Feinberg, 22.
98. Strong, H6822.
99. *Foundation*, 901.
100. Feinberg, 29.
101. *Foundation*, 901.
102. Feinberg, 29.
103. Spurgeon, *Quote Fancy*.
104. Strong, H5975.
105. Dake, 1365.
106. Strong, H6137.
107. Wycliffe, 704.
108. Jamieson, 211.
109. Feinberg, 29.
110. Barnes, 299.
111. "Lives of the Prophets," newworldencyclopedia.org.
112. Strong, H3068.
113. Hayford, 1095.
114. Wycliffe, 711.
115. Strong, H430.
116. Hayford, 1095.
117. Feinberg, 22.
118. Strong, 7200.
119. Strong, 4397.
120. Strong, 3070.
121. Rudd, "Exodus Route," bible.ca/archeology.
122. Strong, H7495.
123. Strong, G2390.
124. Hayford, 1848.
125. Rudd.
126. Hayford, 849.
127. "Billy Graham," azquotes.com.
128. Strong, H3073.
129. Strong, G3339.
130. Hayford, 1908.
131. *Foundation*, 945.

132. Clarkson, "Significance of Palm," biblehub.com.
133. Christian, "14 Roof," dreamchrist.com.
134. Strong, H5572.
135. Strong, G680.
136. "Entry," biblestudytools.com.
137. Strong, H361.
138. Strong, H352.
139. Strong, H4609.
140. Kalu, "What Are the Songs," christianity.com.
141. Kalu.
142. Hayford, 1233.
143. Kalu.
144. Strong H4390.
145. Hayford, 1029.
146. Hayford, 1102.
147. "Pickelhaube," wikipedia.org.
148. "Close Ranks," dictionary.cambridge.org.
149. Hayford, 1094.
150. Abbott, "Got Questions," reasonsforhopejesus.com.
151. "Pioneer," *Webster's New World Dictionary*, 1027.

Appendix #1

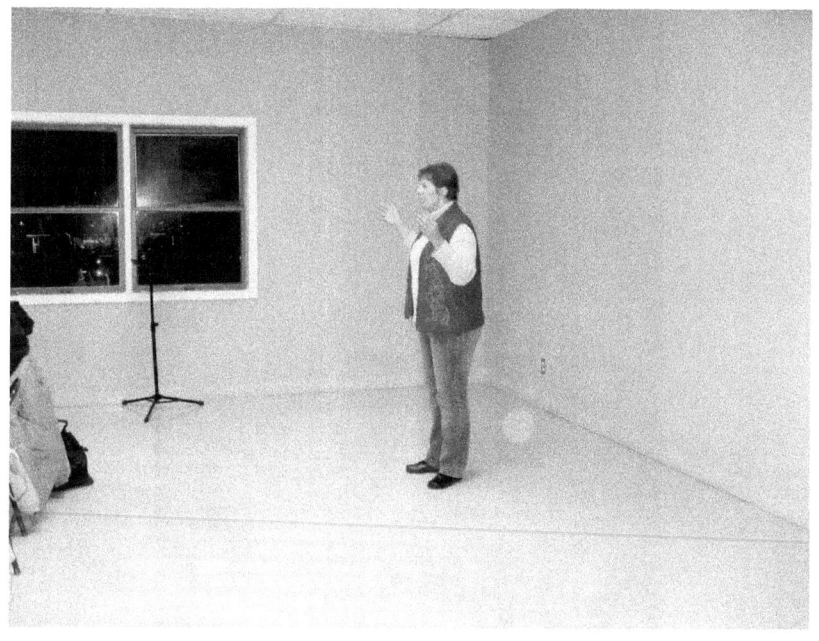

ORBS AT BIBLE STUDY (p. 10)

Appendix #2

BEAMS AFTER WORSHIP (p. 11)

Appendix #3

BEAM WHICH TURNED INTO FLASH OF LIGHT (p. 11)

Appendix #4

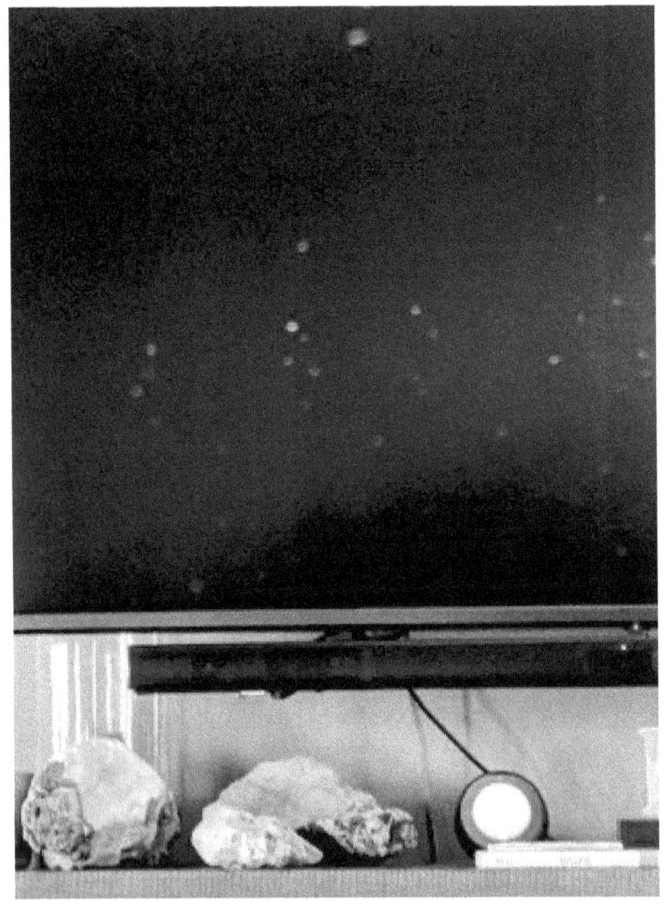

GLITTER IN FRONT OF TELEVISION (p. 11)

Appendix #5

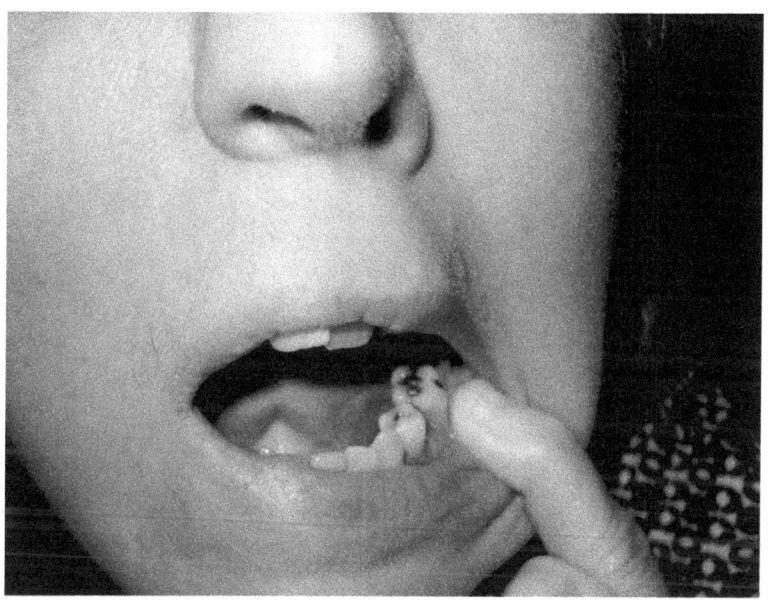

LADY AT BIBLE STUDY RECEIVED GOLD FILLING SHAPED LIKE A CROSS (p. 70)

Appendix #6

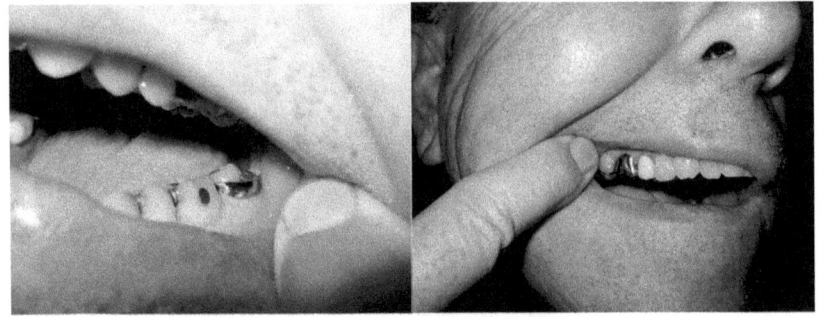

WADE WITH GOLD BRACKETS AND GOLD TOOTH (p. 70)

Appendix #7

RAINBOW OVER HOUSE DURING TONY'S ILLNESS. RAINBOW'S END GOING INTO GARAGE WHERE HE PASSED AWAY (p. 100)

Appendix #8

ORBS TO CELEBRATE TONY'S HEAVENLY HOMECOMING (p. 101)

Appendix #9

KRISTI'S ANGEL FEATHER (p. 102)

Appendix #10

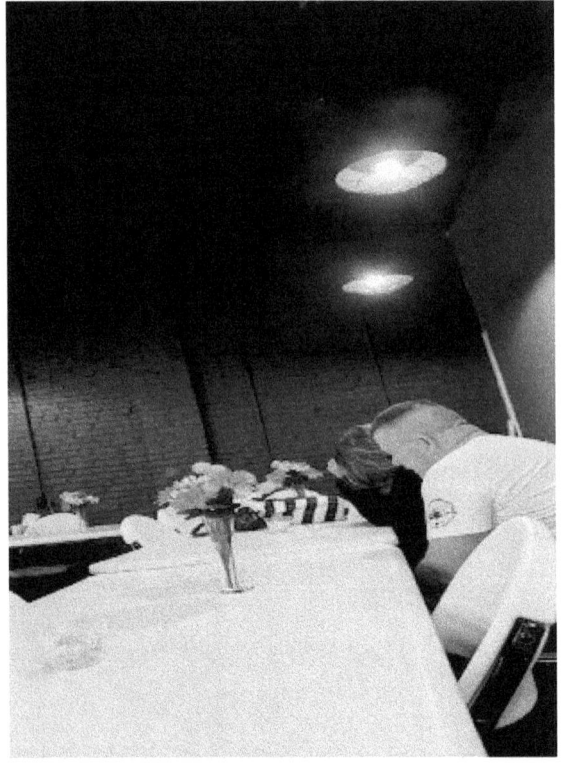

ANGEL WITH YELLOW HAIR ABOVE LIGHT DURING WORSHIP (p. 109)

Appendix #11

BEAM AT MY FEET (p. 110)

Appendix #12

BABY RATTLESNAKE BEFORE IT WAS RELEASED (p. 113)

Bibliography

Abbott, Shari. "Got Questions? What is the Vertical & Horizontal of the Cross?" *Reasons for Hope*Jesus*. 2022. Date accessed 31 Oct. 2022.https://reasonsforhopejesus.com/what-is-the-vertical-and-horizontal-of-the-cross/.

Barnes' Notes on the Old & New Testaments. Cook, F.C., ed. *The Bible Commentary*. Baker Book House, Grand Rapids, Michigan: 1981, Vol. Proverbs-Ezekiel, pp. 299, 307–308, 310–312.

"Billy Graham Quotes About Knowing God." *AZ Quotes*. Twitter post from Jan 14, 2013. https://www.azquotes.com/author/5776-Billy_Graham/tag/knowing-god.

Christian, A. "14 Roof Dream Interpretation." *DreamChrist*. 2022. Date Accessed: 1 Nov. 2022. https://www.dreamchrist.com/roof-dream-interpretation/.

Clarkson, W. "The Significance of the Palm Trees." The Pulpit Commentary, Electronic Database by Biblesoft, Inc. 2001, 2003, 2005, 2006, 2010. 2022. *Bible Hub*. 2004–2022. Date Accessed 7 Nov. 2022. https://biblehub.com/sermons/auth/clarkson/the_significance_of_the_palm_trees.htm.

"Close Ranks." *Cambridge Dictionary*. Cambridge University. 2022. Date Accessed 24-10-22. https://dictionary.cambridge.org/us/dictionary/english/close-ranks.

Cooper, James. "Seraphim, Cherubim and the Four Living Creatures." 2022. Date accessed 5 Nov. 2022. whyangels.com.

Crandall, Rick. "The Hand of the LORD in Scripture." *FaithlifeSermons*. 2022. Access Date 31 Oct. 2022. https://sermons.faithlife.com/sermons/193807-the-hand-of-the-lord-in-scripture.

Dake, Finis Jennings. *Dake's Annotated Reference Bible*. Lawrenceville, GA: Dake. 1999, pp. 1364–1366, 1439.

"Entry for 'ARCH.'" Orr, James, M.A., D.D. General Editor. *International Standard Bible Encyclopedia*. 1915. From M.G. Easton M.A., D.D., *Illustrated Bible Dictionary*, Third Edition, published by Thomas Nelson, 1897. Date Accessed 10 Oct. 22. https://www.biblestudytools.com/dictionary/arch/.

"Ezekiel's Calling and Commission (Ezekiel 2–3)." United Church of God (an International Corporation. Aug. 14–15. 1995–2022. Date accessed 6 Nov. 2022. https://www.ucg.org/bible-study-tools/bible-commentary/bible-commentary-ezekiel-2-3.

Feinberg, Charles Lee. *The Prophecy of Ezekiel: The Glory of the LORD*. Moody. Chicago. 1969, pp. 11–12, 17, 19–20, 22–25, 27, 29–30.

Gordon, Jonathan and Owen Jarus. "What Is the Ark of the Covenant?" *Live Science*. https://www.livescience.com/64932-the-ark-of-the-covenant.html. February 23, 2022 Date Accessed 9 December 2021.

Bibliography

Hayford, Jack W., and D. Litt, et al. *New Spirit Filled Life Bible*. Nashville: Thomas Nelson Bibles, Thomas Nelson, Inc., 2002. "Bottom Note," 114, 1094–1097, 1102, 1142, 1395, 1848, 1908.

Hayford, Jack W., and D. Litt, et al. *New Spirit Filled Life Bible*. Nashville: Thomas Nelson Bibles, Thomas Nelson, Inc., 2002, "The Holy Spirit at Work," 1092.

Hayford, Jack W., and D. Litt, et al. *New Spirit Filled Life Bible*. Nashville: Thomas Nelson Bibles, Thomas Nelson, Inc., 2002, "Word Wealth," 438, 849, 1233, 1029.

"Interpreting Dictionary." *The Holy Bible*. Dugan, Inc. Gordonsville, TN: 1984, pp. 3–4.

Jamieson, Robert, A. R. Fausset, and David Brown. *A Commentary on the Old and New Testaments. Volume Two, Part Two*, "Jeremiah," pp. 203–205, 207–209, 211.

Jarus, Owen. "The Worst Epidemics and Pandemics in History." *LIVE SCIENCE* in cooperation with *All About History*. 21 Oct. 2022. Access date 8-28-2021. www.livescience.com/worst-epidemics-and-pandemics-in-history.html.

Kalu, Madeline. "What Are the Songs of Ascent in the Bible?" *Christianity.com*. 6 Jul. 2021. Salem Web Network. 2022. Date Accessed 8 Oct. 2022. https://www.christianity.com/wiki/bible/what-are-the-songs-of-ascent-in-the-bible.html.

"Lives of the Prophets: Ezekiel." *New World Encyclopedia*. https://www.newworldencyclopedia.org/entry/Lives_of_the_Prophets. Date accessed 27/9/22.

"Meaning of Colors in the Bible Explained." 2019–2022. Date accessed 22 Sept. 2022. *Colors Explained*. Yellow/Gold in the Bible. https://www.colorsexplained.com/meaning-of-colors-in-the-bible.

NKVJ Foundation Study Bible. The Holy Bible. Nashville. Thomas Nelson, 2015, Bottom Note, pp. 898, 901, 945, 1088.

"Pickelhaube." *Wikipedia*. Nov. 13, 2022. Date Accessed 19 Nov. 2022. https://en.wikipedia.org/wiki/Pickelhaube.

"Pioneer." *Webster's New World Dictionary*. Webster's New World Dictionary, a Division of Simon & Schuster, Inc. 1988: 1027.

Rudd, Steve. "The Exodus Route: 22 stops from Mt. Sinai to Kadesh Barnea." *Biblical Archeology: Digging Up Bible Stories*. https://www.bible.ca/archeology/bible-archeology-exodus-route-sinai-kadesh-barnea.htm. Date accessed 27/9/22.

Spurgeon, Charles H. Featured in "Charles H. Spurgeon Quotes." *Quote Fancy*. Date Accessed 7 Nov. 2022.

Strong, James, LL.D., S.T.D. *King James New Strong's Exhaustive Concordance*. Nashville: Thomas Nelson. 2001, G680, G1391, G1588, G2390, G3339, H1697, G2279, G2822, G2999, H352, H361, H430, H2534, H3068, H3070, H3073, H3374, H3519, H4390, H4397, H4609, H5375, H5401, H5572, H5975, H6137, H6822, H6963, H7015, H7200, H7494, H7495, H8068, H8074, H8085.

"What Is the Meaning of Shekinah Glory?" *Christianity.com*. About Christianity.com. Salem Web Network. 2022. Access date 26 Oct. 22. https://www.christianity.com/wiki/christian-terms/what-is-the-meaning-of-shekinah-glory.html.

Wycliffe Bible Commentary, The. Pfeiffer, Charles F. (Old Testament) and Everett F. Harrison, (New Testament) Editors. Moody. Chicago. 1969, pp. 704, 707, 709–711.

www.ingramcontent.com/pod-product-compliance
Lightning Source LLC
Chambersburg PA
CBHW071205160426
43196CB00011B/2204